NORTH CAROLINA
WILDLIFE
VIEWING GUIDE

Charles E. Roe

FALCON PRESS

Acknowledgments

Special thanks for advisory assistance to:

Randall Wilson and Alan Boynton, N.C. Wildlife Resources Commission, Nongame and Endangered Wildlife Program

Harry LeGrand, Jr., and Stephen Hall, N.C. Natural Heritage Program

Members of the North Carolina Wildlife Viewing Guide Steering Committee

---

Author:

Charles E. Roe, Director, North Carolina Natural Heritage Foundation; Coordinator, North Carolina Audubon Council, Raleigh; past coordinator for the N. C. Natural Heritage Program

Project Coordinator:

Kate Davies, Defenders of Wildlife

Special thanks to Ken Taylor, Chief Photographer of *Wildlife in North Carolina*, for supplying more than half of the outstanding photographs appearing in this book.

Front cover photo:

Brown pelican with nestling, Cape Fear River. WALKER GOLDER

Back cover photos:

Catawba rhododendrons on Craggy Dome WILLIAM S. LEA
Red wolf GRADY ALLEN

Contents

One of North Carolina's blackwater streams, the beautiful Black River flows through the wild, largely unchanged coastal plain region. KEN TAYLOR

REGION SIX: WESTERN PIEDMONT

REGION SEVEN: NORTHERN MOUNTAINS

REGION EIGHT: SOUTHERN MOUNTAINS

Carolina Power & Light Company is an electric utility serving more than 835,000 customers in North Carolina. The lands and waters associated with CP&L's facilities are valuable habitat for many species of wildlife. In cooperation with the North Carolina Wildlife Resources Commission, CP&L provides public access to many of these areas so the wildlife may be appreciated by the state's citizens and visitors. Carolina Power & Light Company, 411 Fayetteville Street, P.O. Box 1551, Raleigh, NC 27602.

Duke Power Company, the nation's seventh-largest, investor-owned electric utility company, has a well-earned reputation for protecting the environment while providing a reliable source of power for 1.6 million customers in North and South Carolina. Duke continues a rich tradition of national environmental leadership that has been recognized by a number of state and national conservation organizations. For more information, write or call Duke Power Company, Corporate Communications, P.O. Box 1009, Charlotte, NC 28201-1009, (704) 382-8337.

The North Carolina Wildlife Resources Commission, as the wildlife authority of the state, serves to restore, manage, conserve, regulate, and protect the state's wildlife resources. In recognition of diverse public interests in North Carolina's natural resources, the Commission is sponsoring the Watchable Wildlife Program to increase public awareness and support. Financial support for this program is provided by state tax refund contributions to the North Carolina Nongame and Endangered Wildlife Fund. Contact the North Carolina Wildlife Resources Commission, 512 N. Salisbury Street, Raleigh, NC 27604-1188, (919) 733-7291.

The United States Army is responsible for training soldiers to defend our nation—and at the same time protect a heritage of abundant natural resources on Army lands. The U.S. Army is pleased to support the Watchable Wildlife Program in an effort to develop a national network of wildlife observation sites for the public. For more information, contact DEH, Hunting and Fishing Center, Fort Bragg, NC 28307-5000, (919) 396-7506/7022.

The North Carolina Department of Transportation is responsible for planning, designing, constructing, and maintaining the State's transportation system. The department is dedicated to providing safe, efficient highways while protecting the environment and providing access to the State's many recreational and scenic areas. The North Carolina Official Highway Map is available free of charge at welcome centers and visitor information offices across the State. North Carolina Department of Transportation, P.O. Box 25201, Raleigh, NC 27611, (919) 733-2520.

The U.S. Department of Agriculture Forest Service has a mandate to protect, improve, and wisely use the nation's forest and range resources for multiple purposes to benefit all Americans. The four national forests of North Carolina are sponsors of this program to promote awareness and enjoyment of fish and wildlife on our national forest system lands. National Forests of North Carolina, Post and Otis Streets, Box 2750, Asheville, NC 28802, (704) 257-4200.

The U.S. Fish and Wildlife Service is pleased to support the watchable wildlife effort in furtherance of its mission to preserve, protect, and enhance fish and wildlife resources and their habitats for the use and enjoyment of the American public. U.S. Fish and Wildlife Service, 551-F Pylon Dr., Raleigh, NC 27636, (919) 856-4520.

Defenders of Wildlife is a national, nonprofit organization of more than 80,000 members and supporters dedicated to preserving the natural abundance and diversity of wildlife and its habitat. A one-year membership is $20 and it includes six issues of the bimonthly magazine, *Defenders*. To join or for further information, write or call Defenders of Wildlife, 1244 Nineteenth Street, N. W., Washington, DC 20036. (202) 659-9510

The National Fish and Wildlife Foundation, chartered by Congress to stimulate private giving to conservation, is an independent not-for-profit organization. Using federally funded challenge grants, it forges partnerships between the public and private sectors to conserve the nation's fish, wildlife, and plants.

Other important contributors include:

Grandfather Mountain, Inc.

National Park Service

North Carolina State Museum of Natural Sciences

North Carolina Division of Parks and Recreation

North Carolina Aquarium Society

Introduction

North Carolina is endowed with a rich biological diversity and many magnificent natural areas. These places provide visitors with immense returns in the areas of outdoor recreation and wildlife viewing. Consider a few of North Carolina's natural superlatives:

- The highest mountain summits in eastern America, with eighty-two peaks rising more than 5,000 feet high and the tallest, Mount Mitchell, soaring to 6,684 feet.

- The oldest stand of trees east of the Rockies—1,600-year-old bald cypresses on the Black River.

- Astounding numbers of wintering waterfowl and shorebirds, including more tundra swans than any other state.

- The geologically oldest river in America, the 100-million-year-old New River, flowing from the ancient Appalachian Mountains.

- Over 320 miles of ocean beaches.

- The most extensive bottomland swamp forests in the Mid-Atlantic coastal region.

- The tallest sand dunes in eastern America, the highest of which is the 140-foot Jockey's Ridge dune found on the Outer Banks barrier islands.

- The largest wilderness mountain areas in the Southern Appalachians, including the half-million-acre Great Smoky Mountains National Park and International Biosphere Reserve shared equally with the state of Tennessee.

- The largest granitic cave in North America, Bat Cave.

- One of the richest diversities of animal and plant species among the states in temperate latitudes, with 850 vertebrate animal species and about 5,500 plant species.

North Carolina's natural landscape and wildlife community have changed greatly since colonial times. When explorers like surveyor general John Lawson and botanists William Bartram and Andre Michaux first charted the state, they described vast expanses of hardwood and longleaf pine forests, broken by fire-maintained grasslands and canebrakes, with a rich diversity of wildlife.

Today, most of these habitats have either disappeared or are generally diminished. Half of North Carolina's wetland areas have been lost to development. More than 200 animals and plants are formally designated as endangered, threatened, or special concern. Many others are suffering population declines and habitat degradation. Wildlife are further imperiled by deteriorating air and water quality.

Public and private efforts continue to preserve natural habitats, but much remains to be accomplished to assure the future of North Carolina's natural diversity. The challenge for the 1990s and beyond will be to protect more natural areas, as well as to maintain existing public lands for the benefit of wildlife and people alike. This guide is meant to increase your enjoyment of North Carolina's wildlife. May it also inspire you to help protect its rich, and threatened, natural heritage.

Tundra swans raise their young in the distant north along the Arctic Ocean, but spend their winters in warmer climates. As many as 50,000-60,000 of these majestic birds may be seen in North Carolina. KEN TAYLOR

The Watchable Wildlife Initiative

For many years, sportsmen and other conservationists have been partners in advocating for the protection of North Carolina's rich wildlife heritage. Sportsmen have supported state wildlife programs through license fees and taxes on firearms and fishing equipment. These programs have also benefited non-game species of wildlife by funding habitat enhancement and preservation programs, wildlife management areas, as well as parks, refuges, and preserves.

Hunting is in decline throughout America, and the weakening of this constituency has brought about economic consequences for wildlife and conservation efforts. Less money is available for wildlife just as the threats to wildlife and habitats are becoming most acute.

As part of a much larger effort to offset these revenue losses in the 1990s and beyond, a national initiative known as Watchable Wildlife has emerged. By providing opportunities for people to experience wildlife and by cultivating public interest in wildlife-related activities, programs created under the Watchable Wildlife banner hope to broaden citizen support for conserving our wildlife resources. Public interest in viewing and photographing wildlife has increased dramatically in recent years; the challenge at hand is to transform this interest into greater public responsibility for developing and financing new conservation programs, geared for the entire public, that will guarantee we have wildlife to watch into the next century.

Responding to this challenge, federal and state wildlife management agencies in North Carolina, in partnership with conservation groups, have cooperatively produced the *North Carolina Wildlife Viewing Guide*. The guide is a first step in this effort and will serve as a building block for a more complete state Watchable Wildlife program in the years to come.

The next step—enhancement of viewing sites—is getting under way in North Carolina. Site enhancement will include interpretive signs and guides, trail development, managing of viewing platforms or blinds, and provision of parking and restroom facilities. Not every viewing site found in this book is fully developed yet, but the process has started.

Watchable Wildlife programs can also work to expand our understanding and appreciation of the natural world in all its diversity. Even those species that are not hunted, easily viewed, or photographed play a critical role in the health of other species and, indeed, entire ecosystems. We must work together to assure that our wildlife heritage survives and prospers—for the health and quality of our natural environment and for the enjoyment of ourselves and future generations.

Viewing Hints

The first and last hours of daylight are generally the best times to view or photograph most animals. Wildlife viewing is usually poor during the heat of a summer day.

Be quiet. Quick movements and loud noises will normally scare wildlife. Since your car or boat can be a good viewing blind, you may actually see more by remaining in your vehicle. Notice how more often you see animals when you are still, than when you are moving. Whisper when you speak.

Binoculars or spotting scopes are always helpful to enhance your observations. Field guides assist with identification and other pertinent facts. Polarized glasses help reduce glare.

Be patient. Wait quietly for animals to enter or return to an area. Give yourself enough time to allow animals to move within your view. Patience is

Beavers are secretive creatures and best seen around twilight. It's not difficult, however, to find evidence of beaver activity around streams and ponds. KEVIN ADAMS

This sign marks a nesting tree for the endangered red-cockaded woodpecker. These birds depend upon old longleaf and loblolly pine forest for their nesting cavities. Habitat destruction is the most common threat to native plants and animals. KEVIN ADAMS

often rewarded with a more complete wildlife experience.

You can further enhance your viewing trips by learning about migration patterns of wildlife, especially birds. In North Carolina, you are more likely to see waterfowl, shorebirds, and raptors during spring and fall migrations, when they visit the state in large numbers. Spring and summer are better times to view many animals such as songbirds, small mammals, deer, and amphibians.

Outdoor Ethics

Honor the rights of private landowners. Gain permission of private landowners before entering their property.

Honor wildlife's requirement of free movement. Feeding, touching, or otherwise harassing wildlife is inappropriate. Young wild animals that appear to be alone have not been abandoned; allow them to find their own way.

Honor the rights of others to enjoy their viewing experience. Loud noises, quick movements, or erratic behavior that might scare wildlife is inappropriate.

Honor your own right to enjoy the outdoors in the future. Leave wildlife habitat in better condition than you found it. Pick up litter that you encounter and dispose of it properly.

How To Use This Guide

The ninety wildlife viewing **sites** are grouped according to the eight travel regions of the state. The **color bars** on the edge of the pages are keyed to each region. Each travel region begins with a **map** displaying all viewing sites by number.

Each **site description** includes featured wildlife and habitats. Additional information is provided to note wildlife viewing probabilities, best viewing seasons, and specific advice related to viewing opportunities. NOTES OF CAUTION RELATING TO ROAD CONDITIONS, SAFETY, VIEWING LIMITATIONS, AND OTHER RESTRICTIONS APPEAR IN CAPITAL LETTERS.

Site **directions** are based on the official North Carolina highway map. **Roads** are identified based on federal or state highway numbers or state secondary road numbers. Towns named on the state highway map are listed as the **closest town**. Viewers are advised to supplement this guide with an official state map and with a privately-published county map book.

Ownership refers to the agency or group that owns or manages a viewing site. The names of private owners or organizations are not always listed. A few private sites have been included in this book with permission of the landowners. Please respect their rights when visiting these sites.

The **phone number** listed after ownership is the number to use if you need more information concerning individual sites. This is usually the managing agency or individual owner.

Each site description also displays **symbols** for wildlife most likely to be seen there. **Recreational icons** are listed to indicate facilities at each site. Facilities are listed only if they are found on the site. In some cases, hotels, restrooms, and other facilities may be nearby.

Featured Wildlife

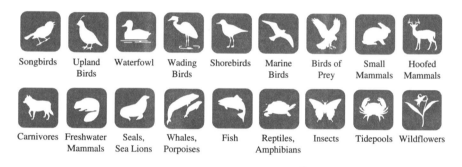

| Songbirds | Upland Birds | Waterfowl | Wading Birds | Shorebirds | Marine Birds | Birds of Prey | Small Mammals | Hoofed Mammals |

| Carnivores | Freshwater Mammals | Seals, Sea Lions | Whales, Porpoises | Fish | Reptiles, Amphibians | Insects | Tidepools | Wildflowers |

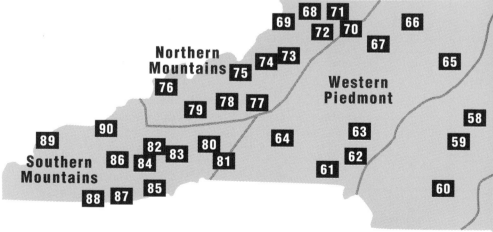

Map Information

North Carolina is divided into eight travel regions shown on this map. Wildlife viewing sites in this guide are numbered consecutively in a general pattern. Each region forms a separate section in this book, and each section begins with a map of that region.

1 This symbol indicates the location and number of a wildlife viewing site.

Facilities and Recreation

P Parking

🚻 Restrooms

🍴 Restaurant

🛏 Lodging

$ Fee

⛱ Picnic

🏃 Trails

⛰ Camping

🚲 Bicycling

🛶 Small Boats

🚣 Boat Ramp

🚤 Large Boats

⛷ Cross-country Skiing

♿ Handicap Accessible

Highway Signs

As you travel across North Carolina, look for these special highway signs that identify wildlife viewing sites. Most signs show the binoculars logo or the words "Wildlife Viewing Area," often with an arrow pointing toward the site.

Site Owner/Manager Abbreviations

USFS U.S. Forest Service
NPS   National Park Service
TNC   The Nature Conservancy
PVT   Private ownership

USFWS U.S. Fish and Wildlife Service
NCDPR N.C. Division of Parks & Recreation
NCWRC Wildlife Resources Commission
NCDFR N.C. Division of Forest Resources

NCDCM   N.C. Division of Coastal Management

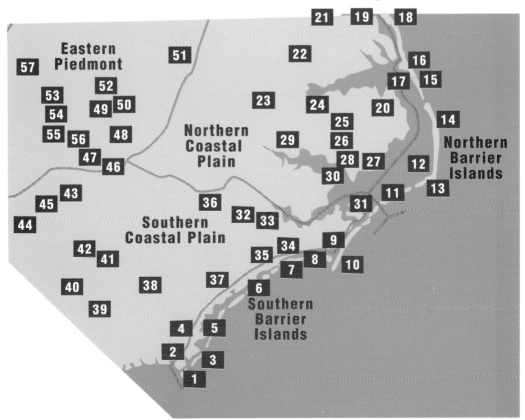

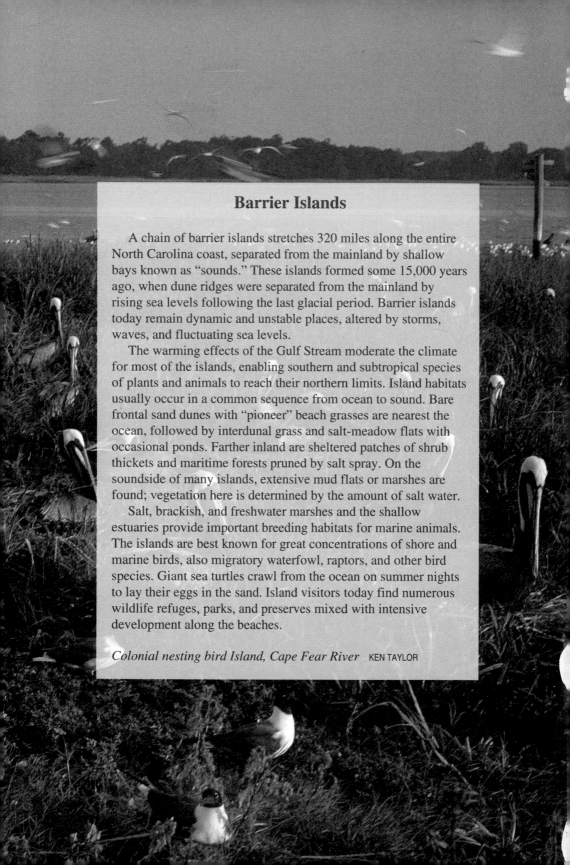

Barrier Islands

A chain of barrier islands stretches 320 miles along the entire North Carolina coast, separated from the mainland by shallow bays known as "sounds." These islands formed some 15,000 years ago, when dune ridges were separated from the mainland by rising sea levels following the last glacial period. Barrier islands today remain dynamic and unstable places, altered by storms, waves, and fluctuating sea levels.

The warming effects of the Gulf Stream moderate the climate for most of the islands, enabling southern and subtropical species of plants and animals to reach their northern limits. Island habitats usually occur in a common sequence from ocean to sound. Bare frontal sand dunes with "pioneer" beach grasses are nearest the ocean, followed by interdunal grass and salt-meadow flats with occasional ponds. Farther inland are sheltered patches of shrub thickets and maritime forests pruned by salt spray. On the soundside of many islands, extensive mud flats or marshes are found; vegetation here is determined by the amount of salt water.

Salt, brackish, and freshwater marshes and the shallow estuaries provide important breeding habitats for marine animals. The islands are best known for great concentrations of shore and marine birds, also migratory waterfowl, raptors, and other bird species. Giant sea turtles crawl from the ocean on summer nights to lay their eggs in the sand. Island visitors today find numerous wildlife refuges, parks, and preserves mixed with intensive development along the beaches.

Colonial nesting bird Island, Cape Fear River KEN TAYLOR

SOUTHERN BARRIER ISLANDS

SITE NUMBER	SITE NAME
1	Bald Head Island
2	Battery Island and Cape Fear River Islands
3	Fort Fisher State Recreation Area
4	Carolina Beach State Park
5	Masonboro Island
6	Hammocks Beach State Park
7	Theodore Roosevelt Natural Area
8	Fort Macon State Park
9	Rachel Carson Estuarine Research Reserve
10	Cape Lookout National Seashore

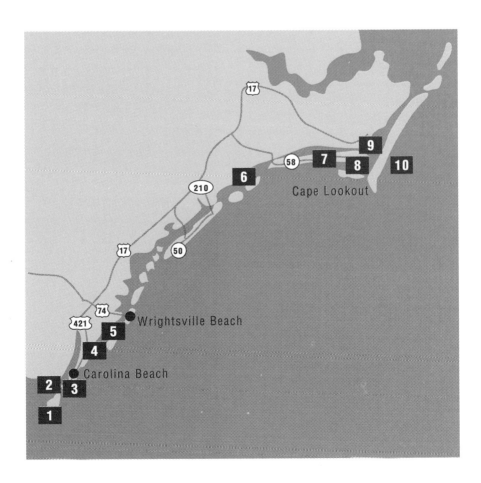

1 Bald Head Island

Description: A barrier island complex of ocean beaches, dunes, maritime forests, freshwater ponds, tidal creeks, salt marshes, lagoons, estuaries, and mudflats. Maritime forests are semi-tropical, dominated by live oak, laurel oak, loblolly pine, and palmetto trees. Site of state's largest nesting population of loggerhead sea turtles. These 300-pound reptiles come ashore in the summer to lay more than 100 nests on the beaches. Brown pelicans are year-round residents often seen feeding along shore. Many species of shorebirds and waterfowl on expansive intertidal flats. Watch for giant swallowtails and other southern butterflies.

Viewing Information: Viewing of seashore wildlife throughout the island complex is accessible by boat and beach hiking. Contact the Bald Head Corporation (919-457-5003) for ferry tickets or marina use. Bald Head Island Conservancy (919-457-7350 for reservations) leads summer night vigils to see sea turtles nest and hatch. Electric carts are the only vehicles allowed on beaches (919-457-4944 for cart rental). The island is isolated and subject to storms.

Directions: Private passenger ferry services from Southport on mainland. Private boat access from Cape Fear River or Fort Fisher landings. Walkers can reach the Zeke's Island National Estuarine Research Reserve (at northern end of Bald Head complex) at low tide via the rock breakwater from Fort Fisher State Recreation Area.

Ownership: Bald Head Corporation (919-457-5000), NCDCM (919-256-3721), NCWRC (919-733-7291), NCDPR (919-458-8206)

Size: 10,000 acres   **Closest Towns:** Southport and Bald Head

The reward for a sleepless night on a beach is the chance to witness a 350- to 1,000-pound loggerhead turtle crawling from the sea to make her nest. North Carolina hosts as many as 800 sea turtle nests every year. KEN TAYLOR

2 **Battery Island and Cape Fear River Islands**

Description: Several islands in the Cape Fear River near Southport serve as breeding sites for the state's largest colony of wading birds. Large colonies of brown pelicans, gulls, and terns may also be seen. Several thousand herons, egrets, and ibises nest in shrub thickets on the Battery Island Audubon Sanctuary, for many years the state's largest colony of these birds. Nearby Ferry Slip and South Pelican Islands harbor over 500 nesting pairs of brown pelicans and large numbers of nesting gulls and terns.

Viewing Information: Viewing from boats best in late spring and summer. No foot access permitted from March to September due to birds' nesting season. Binoculars necessary to see birds from offshore boats. DO NOT SET FOOT ON THE ISLANDS (patrolled regularly by wardens).

Directions: Private boat access from public landing on Southport waterfront.

Ownership: Battery Island state-owned but managed by National Audubon Society (919-256-3779); other islands owned by NCWRC (919-733-7291)

Size: Battery Island 100 acres, Ferry Slip and Pelican Islands less than ten acres

Closest Town: Southport

South Pelican Island, located near Southport, is a haven for nesting shorebirds such as pelicans, herons, egrets, and terns. More than twenty-three species of shorebirds nest along the state's coastline. JAMES F. PARNELL

3 Fort Fisher State Recreation Area

Description: Full range of seashore wildlife observable along the Fort Fisher barrier island spit, extending 3.7 miles south from the state's historic fort site. Recreation area contains ocean beach, dunes, shrub thickets, salt marshes, and tidepools. Nearby North Carolina Aquarium offers interpretive exhibits, programs, and tours. Visitors may see a diversity of resident and migrant birds, many other coastal animals, and teeming invertebrate life in marshes and tidepools.

Viewing Information: Self-guided nature trails from Aquarium. Boardwalks through shrub thickets, marsh, and frontal dunes to beach. Sheltered deck near beach. Beach swimming and fishing. Historic rock jetty leads to national estuarine research reserve at northern end of Bald Head Island. Beach access on designated paths allowed for off-road vehicles. Access to shorebird nesting sites may be restricted.

Directions: From Wilmington travel south on U.S. 421, through Carolina Beach and Kure Beach, and past Fort Fisher Historic Site. Paved access road (SR 1713) to Aquarium and Recreation Area. From Southport take public toll ferry.

Ownership: NCDPR (919-458-8206), NCDCM (919-256-3721), NC Aquarium (919-458-8257)

Size: 300 acres   **Closest Towns:** Kure Beach and Southport

A flock of beautiful black skimmers seen at Fort Fisher State Recreation Area.
WALKER GOLDER

4 Carolina Beach State Park

Description: Borders the Cape Fear River. Carolina Beach features a series of sand ridges, dunes, and swales typical of barrier islands. Varied forest habitats, swamps, savannas, limesink ponds, and brackish tidal marsh harbor diverse wildlife. Good location for bird watching with habitats for abundant resident land species and refuge for many migrant species of warblers, finches, sparrows, and hawks, especially in the fall. Watch in summer for summer tanagers, chuck-will's widows, Swainson's warblers, and painted buntings. Uncommon amphibians and reptiles such as Carolina gopher frog and alligator. Green treefrogs and Carolina anole lizards commonly seen.

Viewing Information: More than five miles of winding foot trails, including an interpretive nature trail loop from parking lots. Good year-round wildlife viewing. Interpretive natural history programs offered during summer season.

Directions: From Wilmington, go ten miles south on U.S. 421. Turn west on park access road, located south of Snows Cut Bridge and on the north side of town of Carolina Beach.

Ownership: NCDPR (919-458-8206)

Size: 420 acres   **Closest Town:** Carolina Beach

5 Masonboro Island

Description: Nine-mile-long island designated a national estuarine reserve and characteristic of narrow, low barrier islands along the state's southern coast. Low-elevation island frequently subject to storm overwash and vulnerable to beach erosion and inlet formation. Behind the island are extensive salt marshes, tidal flats, and a shallow sound. Behind the frontal sand dunes are grassy flats, maritime shrub thickets, tidal creeks, and mudflats. Island is important habitat for nesting waterbirds such as least and royal terns, willets, black skimmers, and oystercatchers. Wide variety of other seashore wildlife. Beach nesting by loggerhead sea turtles in summer.

Viewing Information: Access by small private boat and occasional organized tours. Beach access may be restricted near nesting colonies of shorebirds. No vehicles allowed on beach. WATCH FOR SIGNS AND BARRIERS AND STAY AWAY FROM NESTING SHOREBIRDS.

Directions: Private boat access from public launch sites on the mainland or Wrightsville Beach to the north.

Ownership: NCDCM (919-256-3721)

Size: 5,000 acres   **Closest Towns:** Topsail, Wrightsville Beach

6 | Hammocks Beach State Park

Description: State park on an undeveloped barrier island 3.5 miles long. Shorebirds, waterfowl, and marine life are abundant in salt marshes, tidal creeks, and frontal beach dunes. Large mobile sand dunes up to sixty feet high cover island's maritime forests. Large numbers of sea turtles nest on beaches in summer. Osprey and brown pelicans feed in the marshes and surf. Least terns, black skimmers, and common terns nest on island along with willets, oystercatchers, and other shorebirds. Fall brings large flocks of migratory warblers, sparrows, and hawks. Tracks of gray fox, raccoon, and deer common along the beach. Look in sand for tracks of the ant lion. Lizards and non-poisonous snakes commonly seen. A rich variety of marine life may be viewed in marshes and tidal creeks.

Viewing Information: Public access limited to capacity of park passenger ferries from mainland during spring and summer. Private boat landings allowed. Island open to access by foot. No vehicles allowed on island. Beach shelters, interpretive center, swimming beach and shower house. On the ferry ride between mainland and island, look for egrets, herons, ibises, willets, oystercatchers, osprey, rails, and terrapins.

Directions: Reach the park's ferry landing on mainland, from Swansboro west one mile on NC 24; turn south on SR 1511 at park sign and continue 2.3 miles to ferry docks.

Ownership: NCDPR (919-326-4881)

Size: 736 acres   **Closest Town:** Swansboro

Coastal salt marshes at Hammocks Beach State Park. These wetland areas are some of the most productive ecosystems, providing habitat for scores of animals, including birds, small mammals, and fish. KEN TAYLOR/N.C.WILDLIFE

Description: Remnant maritime forest, now surrounded by urban development, contains natural habitats once prevalent over most of Bogue Banks island. On the dune ridges is a tangled forest of live and laurel oaks, loblolly pine, red cedar, yaupon, and wax myrtle "pruned" by salt spray. Interdunal swales contain swamp forest and freshwater marshes. Salt and brackish marsh border Bogue Sound. The North Carolina Pine Knoll Shores Aquarium is located in the nature preserve. Bird life is abundant, including many warblers, vireos, thrushes, kinglets, and other songbirds in the forest. Wading birds like egrets are found in marshes, with osprey and other raptors hunting overhead.

Viewing Information: Good year-round viewing of forest wildlife, especially resident and migratory birds, small mammals, reptiles, and amphibians. Loop nature trails and boardwalks lead from the aquarium, which offers many interesting exhibits, programs, and tours. Soundside wildlife observation deck. In nearby Salter Path, a tract of protected beach habitat managed by the Aquarium has public beach access parking and boardwalk.

Directions: Take Atlantic Beach bridge south from U.S. 70 in Morehead City. On Bogue Banks island drive west seven miles from Atlantic Beach or east from Salter Path on NC 58. Turn north on paved access road, Pine Knoll Blvd; then first left on Roosevelt Drive as marked to preserve and aquarium.

Ownership: NCDPR (919-762-3775), NC Aquarium (919-247-4003)

Size: 265 acres   **Closest Town:** Pine Knoll Shores   P ⏚ ⤢ ⚲

The white ibis is easily identified by its long, curving bill. Barrier islands provide critical nesting habitat for these and other shorebirds. WALKER GOLDER

21

8 Fort Macon State Park

Description: A Civil War fortress located on the easternmost tip of Bogue Banks island overlooking Beaufort Inlet. Excellent opportunities here to see abundant coastal wildlife: a diversity of year-round resident bird species, wintering flocks of warblers, sparrows, and other migrants, and occasional regional rarities. Terns, gulls, sanderlings, and dunlin frequent the beaches. In winter look for loons, cormorants, and mergansers in the inlet. Racerunner lizards common in the dunes. Bottle-nosed dolphins seen offshore in all seasons. Occasional beach nesting by sea turtles. Rich abundance of invertebrate life in marshes and tidepools, including sea stars, corals, and sea urchins.

Viewing Information: Easy quarter-mile loop nature trail from fort parking lot. Fort open for tours year-round. Beach swimming and fishing. Bathhouse and picnic shelters.

Directions: Take Atlantic Beach bridge south from U.S. 70 in Morehead City. On Bogue Banks island turn east on SR 1190 in Atlantic Beach; entrance on eastern end of the island.

Ownership: NCDPR (919-762-3775)

Size: 389 acres   **Closest Town:** Atlantic Beach

P 🏠 🛪 👤 ♿

9 Rachel Carson National Estuarine Research Reserve

Description: This national estuarine research reserve includes Carrot, Horse, and Bird Shoal islands, and Town Marsh. Habitats include low shrub-covered islands, intertidal flats, and salt marshes. View a high diversity of wildlife here, including more than 200 bird species such as terns, piping plover, oystercatcher, osprey, northern harrier, white ibis, pelican, double-crested cormorant, and red-throated loon. A small herd of feral horses roams the islands.

Viewing Information: Easily seen across Taylor's Creek from historic town of Beaufort and Duke University Marine Lab. Private boat access. Guided tours from North Carolina Maritime Museum on Beaufort's Front Street, which also has exhibits on coastal natural and cultural history. Self-guided interpretive trails under development

Directions: Boat access from Beaufort waterfront. Public boat ramp at east end of Front Street. Reach town waterfront from U.S. 70.

Ownership: NCDCM (919-728-2170)

Information from North Carolina Maritime Museum: (919-728-7317)

Size: 2,025 acres   **Closest Town:** Beaufort

Description: A fifty-six mile stretch of three undeveloped barrier islands separated from mainland by open-water sounds. North and South Core Banks are narrow, low-lying islands with extensive beach berms and interdunal sand flats covered by grasses and shrubs. Tree-covered hammocks and salt marshes extend along the sound. Cape Lookout, location of a 19th century lighthouse, forms a dramatic point jutting into the ocean. Shackleford Banks, unlike islands north of the Cape, is oriented east-west, perpendicular to prevailing winds, and boasts a greater variety of animals and plants. Its higher dunes deflect overwash and salt spray, allowing an extensive maritime forest. Shackleford also has permanent freshwater ponds and marshes supporting a great variety of wildlife. All the islands host numerous shorebirds and nesting sea turtles. Tidal flats are favored by gulls, terns, skimmers, and wading birds. During migrations view a diversity of shorebirds. Cape Lookout point is a good place to see pelagic birds.

Viewing Information: Toll ferries carry passengers and off-road beach vehicles from several mainland access points. Private boats allowed on islands. Most popular destinations for day visitors are the Cape Lookout lighthouse, Shackleford Banks wilderness, and Portsmouth historic village area. National Park Service maintains a visitors center and interpretive programs. NC Maritime Museum provides weekend programs. OBEY SIGNS THAT PROHIBIT ENTRY INTO SHOREBIRD NESTING SITES.

Directions: National seashore reached from boat launches in Beaufort, Harkers Island, Davis, and Atlantic on the mainland, or from Ocracoke Island. Park ranger station on Harkers Island.

Ownership: USNPS (919-240-1409)

Size: 23,780 acres   **Closest Town:** Beaufort

When you see butterflies such as this tiger swallowtail, it's a good bet that wildflowers are nearby.
MELISSA McGAW/N.C. WILDLIFE

23

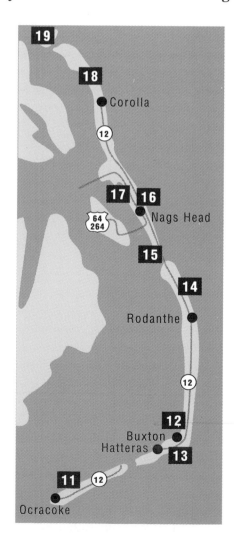

11 | Cape Hatteras National Seashore: Ocracoke Island

Description: Large numbers of terns, skimmers, brown pelicans, cormorants, also many gulls, sandpipers, and other shorebirds nest and feed along the twelve miles of beaches on this southernmost island, one of the chain of barrier islands in Cape Hatteras National Seashore. On this island's eastern tip, piping plovers nest on sand flats, while ducks and shorebirds frequent a small pond near the ferry terminal. Secretive rails inhabit the marshes. Racerunner lizards often seen on dunes. The vegetation zones here are typical of narrow barrier island.

Viewing Information: Frequent wildlife viewing opportunites along the highway and beach; view waterfowl and shorebirds from public ferries crossing Pamlico Sound between Ocracoke and the Swanquarter or Cedar Island terminals on the mainland. Numerous paved pulloffs and parking areas for beach and sound access. Interpretive nature trail on soundside near NPS campground. Beaches open to off-road vehicles. ACCESS RESTRICTIONS IN SHOREBIRD NESTING AREAS; OBEY WARNING SIGNS.

Directions: Island is transected by NC 12. Ferries transport passengers and vehicles to both ends of the island south from Cedar Island, Swan Quarter on the mainland (toll ferries, 2.25 hours passage), and from Hatteras Island on the north (free ferry, forty-minute passage). Town of Ocracoke located near island's southwestern end.

Ownership: NPS (919-473-2111)

Size: 5,500 acres   **Closest Town:** historic village of Ocracoke

The spotted sandpiper makes its summer home in the far reaches of the arctic, and spends the winter in South America. Between destinations, the bird is seen making rest stops along the Carolina coast.

JAMES F. PARNELL

12 | Cape Hatteras National Seashore: Hatteras Island

Description: Cape Hatteras is famed for great concentrations of migratory birds on the Atlantic Flyway. Nearly 400 species of birds have been sighted within the national seashore and adjacent waters. Birdwatching is best during the spring and fall migrations. Look for landbirds in shrub thickets and maritime forests. Largest concentrations of wintering ducks and geese are in large ponds and salt marshes on Pea Island and Bodie Island. Terns, plovers, and skimmers nest in low dunes. Herons, egrets, terns, skimmers, and other breeding birds best seen in warmer months. Beach nesting by loggerhead sea turtles in summer.

Viewing Information: Paved parking pulloffs along NC 12 throughout the length of national seashore; provide access to both beach and sound viewing. PARK ONLY ON DESIGNATED PAVED PULLOFFS; VEHICLES MAY EASILY BECOME STUCK IN SAND. Beach access provided to off-road vehicles. LISTEN TO WEATHER REPORTS AND BE PREPARED TO EVACUATE ISLAND IN EVENT OF STORM. ACCESS RESTRICTIONS AROUND SHOREBIRD NESTING AREAS; OBEY WARNING SIGNS.

Directions: NC 12 runs length of the island, with frequent parking pulloffs. Reached by free public ferry from Ocracoke Island on the south. Bonner Bridge spans Oregon Inlet on north end of Hatteras island.

Ownership: NPS (919-473-2111)/PVT

Size: Island fifty miles long

Closest towns: Hatteras, Frisco, Buxton, Avon, and Rodanthe communities on the island

Expert anglers, great cormorants are often seen diving for fish in the state's coastal waters. Most cormorants are winter residents.
WILLIAM S. LEA

Description: Largest surviving maritime forest on North Carolina barrier islands. A diverse resident population of wildlife, with visits by migratory birds. Woods and interdunal freshwater marshes offer variety of habitats. The forest shelters many warblers, sparrows, vireos, thrushes, flycatchers, and other birds that migrate along the Atlantic coast in spring and fall. Large numbers of raptors, especially migrating hawks. Cape Point excellent for viewing resident and migratory shorebirds and occasional pelagic birds. Large colonies of terns and black skimmers nest near the large tidal pond on Cape Point. Small numbers of the threatened piping plover nest in the dunes. Thousands of terns, gulls, and other shore and waterbirds forage and rest on the cape's sand beaches and ponds, along with smaller numbers of ducks and geese. Freshwater ponds near the historic Hatteras Lighthouse feature yellow-bellied sliders and other turtles, frogs, and fish. Watch for giant swallowtails and other maritime butterflies.

Viewing Information: Interpretive nature trails from parking lots near park visitor center and campground. Good year-round wildlife viewing, but best in fall and spring.

Directions: *Turn toward Cape Hatteras lighthouse and park visitor center on marked access road from NC 12 in town of Buxton.*

Ownership: NPS (919-473-2111), NCDCM (919-256-3721), Friends of Hatteras land trust (919-995-5055)

Size: 2,600 acres   **Closest Town:** Buxton

Laughing gulls nest along the North Carolina coast, but usually winter farther south. They are often seen with other gulls.
KEN TAYLOR

14 Pea Island National Wildlife Refuge

Description: This refuge on the northern section of Hatteras Island contains representative barrier island and estuarine habitats that host many thousands of snow and Canada geese, tundra swans, and twenty-five species of ducks. Immense populations of waterfowl spend the winter here. Counts of 265 regularly seen bird species and fifty species of uncommon birds. View migrating raptors in fall, including many hawks and owls. Peregrine falcons frequently observed and bald eagles occasionally seen during migrations. Nesting colonies of herons, egrets, and ibises. Thousands of shorebirds seen on island ponds, especially in fall. Abundant snapping turtles and other turtles in ponds. Resident mammals include otter and muskrat. Many species of aquatic life in marshes and along the sound. Nesting by loggerhead sea turtles on thirteen miles of ocean beach. Refuge actively managed to enhance wildlife habitats.

Viewing Information: Best wildlife viewing in fall and winter. Frequent parking pullovers and observation platforms along roadway, with footpaths for beach access. Half-mile self-guided nature trail and four-mile observation trail around North Pond impoundment. Refuge interpretive stations. Beach driving not allowed in refuge. DO NOT PULL OFF ROAD INTO DEEP SAND; PARK ONLY IN DESIGNATED PAVED PULLOFFS.

Directions: *Located on north end of Hatteras Island immediately south of the Bonner Bridge over Oregon Inlet, north of village of Rodanthe. NC 12 runs length of the island.*

Ownership: USFWS (919-987-2394)

Size: 5,915 acres of barrier island and 25,700 acres of Pamlico Sound

Closest Town: Rodanthe

P 🚻 🥾

Pea Island National Wildlife Refuge features a four-mile observation trail and a half-mile self-guided nature trail. As many as 265 species of birds are seen here regularly. KEVIN ADAMS

15 Cape Hatteras National Seashore: Bodie Island Lighthouse

Description: On soundside of Coquina Beach, the entrance drive to Bodie Island Lighthouse and visitor center passes through pines and shrubs often crowded in fall by warblers, thrushes, and other landbird migrants. From the visitor center, walk the loop nature trail to observation platforms over fresh marshes and pond to see dabbling ducks, tundra swans, herons and egrets, rails, gulls, and shorebirds. Favorite hunting ground for hawks and falcons. Marsh and shrub thickets often loaded with marsh and sedge wrens, swamp sparrows, yellowthroats, and towhees. From lighthouse north three miles to park entrance, ponds and marshes on island's soundside host many gulls, terns, herons and egrets, wintering snow geese, other waterfowl, shorebirds, rails, and other marsh birds. Watch for marsh rabbits and cottontails.

Viewing Information: Interpretive nature trail, with boardwalk and observation decks leading from visitor center and lighthouse through marshes, shrub thickets, and margin of open pond. Pullovers, observation platforms, and footpaths lead from NC 12 north of lighthouse to viewing sites over soundside marshes and ponds.

Directions: *South from Nags Head about five miles on NC 12 (north of Oregon Inlet marina and bridge) on soundside from Coquina Beach, next to Bodie Is. Lighthouse and Visitor Center.*

Ownership: NPS (919-473-2111)
Size: 255 acres   **Closest Town:** Nags Head

16 Jockey's Ridge State Park

Description: Site of tallest and most active sand dune on the eastern Atlantic Coast. Dune varies from 110 to 140 feet in height, depending on wind conditions. The bare dune, maritime shrub thickets, and woods at its base are rich wildlife habitats. Along with many migratory birds, visitors may see numerous animals and many animal tracks—gray fox, white-tailed deer, rabbits, racerunner lizards, beetles—especially in the early mornings and evenings. The forest and marshes west of dune provide the best habitat. Large numbers of migratory birds can be seen in flight; waterfowl often present on sound in winter.

Viewing Information: Park natural history museum/interpretive center and 1.5 mile-long, self-guided nature trail marked from parking lot. Interpretive boardwalk leads through shrub thickets.

Directions: *Turn west off U.S. 158 bypass at milepost 12 on soundside of Nags Head at park entrance.*

Ownership: NCDPR (919-441-7132)
Size: 414 acres   **Closet Town:** Nags Head

17 Nags Head Woods

Description: Spectacular assemblage of mature maritime forests, relict sand dunes, freshwater ponds, pine-covered hummocks, and expanses of fresh and brackish marshes provide habitats for a great variety of animal life. Sheltered old-growth forest is dominated by large hardwood trees. Numerous hawks, songbirds including the beautiful prothonotary warbler, wood ducks, and wading birds. Look for pileated and other woodpeckers. Important refuge for migrant songbirds in both fall and spring. Deer, otter, muskrats, and other mammals roam the woods. Ponds harbor reptiles and amphibians, including marbled and red-backed salamanders, pine woods snake, and many turtles.

Viewing Information: Numerous self-guided nature trails within the preserve. Trail information available at preserve visitors center. Preserve open limited hours; check first by calling 919-441-2525.

Directions: Turn west from U.S. 158 bypass at North Ocean Dr. approximately one mile south from Wright Brothers NPS First Flight Memorial and two miles north from Jockeys Ridge State Park; follow access road one mile (becomes a sand road) through residential neighborhood to visitor center at edge of preserve.

Ownership: TNC (919-441-2525), Towns of Nags Head and Kill Devil Hills, PVT

Size: Approximately 1,600 acres

Closest Towns: Nags Head and Kill Devil Hills

P🏕🏠🚶

Small but ferocious predators, mink in North Carolina feed primarily on fish. Mink inhabit wetland marsh areas and may also prey on muskrats.
PARIS TRAIL

Brown pelicans are a common sight along the North Carolina coast. These majestic birds were nearly eliminated from the state due to high levels of DDT and other toxins in the food chain. Increased regulation of pesticides and habitat protection efforts have enabled brown pelican populations to soar again.
WALKER GOLDER

18 | Currituck Banks

Description: This twenty-two-mile stretch of barrier island and sound waters includes national wildlife refuge, nature preserve, and estuarine research reserve. Diverse, protected habitats here make the Currituck Outer Banks and Sound one of the richest areas for migratory waterfowl in the Atlantic flyway. Thousands of diving and puddle ducks, geese, and swans use the marshes during fall and winter. Large numbers of migrating land birds and raptors including hawks, peregrine falcons, and bald eagles pass through during fall. Osprey are regular nesters. Currituck Banks are famous for winter concentrations of snow geese and tundra swans. Resident wildlife is also abundant. Watch for mammals, reptiles and amphibians. Large heron nesting colony on Monkey Island. Occasional beach nesting by loggerhead sea turtles.

Viewing Information: NO PAVED ROADS NORTH FROM COROLLA. Beach access from Corolla to hikers and off-road beach vehicles. Research reserve is located immediately north of town. Private boat access to wildlife refuge. County is restoring the Whalehead Club hunting lodge near historic lighthouse in Corolla as visitors center with exhibits about the island's wildlife and cultural resources.

Directions: Research reserve and refuge located north of Corolla from terminus of NC 12.

Additional Viewing Opportunities: National Audubon Society's Pine Island Sanctuary (5,221 acres south of Corolla) on soundside of Currituck Banks is closed to visiting public except by special reservation. A two-mile nature trail with platforms overlooking marshes is open to the public. For more information call 919-453-2838.

Ownership: USFWS (919-429-3100), NCDCM (919-256-3721), National Audubon Society (919-453-2838), TNC and Currituck County

Size: Approximately 13,000 acres protected   **Closest Town:** Corolla

This gray tree frog is all but invisible when perched on a stalk of grass. Many smaller creatures depend on protective coloration to elude predators. Wildlife watchers must look carefully to spot such reclusive animals. KEN TAYLOR/N.C. WILDLIFE

19 Mackay Island National Wildlife Refuge

Description: Thousands of ducks, geese, and swans flock to the refuge's brackish marshes and water areas for the winter. The island's needlerush marshes and young forests in the northern end of Currituck Sound offer habitat for great numbers of migratory waterfowl. Wintering populations have exceeded 50,000 snow geese, 4,000 tundra swans, and many duck species. Osprey, owls, and other raptors hunt and nest. Along with other resident animals, more than 180 species of birds observed such as rails, bitterns, marsh wrens, herons and egrets, flocks of red-winged blackbirds, warblers, and other songbirds.

Viewing Information: Several roadside observation facilities and foot trails in the refuge. The Great Marsh Trail is .3-mile loop from a parking pulloff along Knotts Island Causeway (NC 615); foot trail winds through marshes, freshwater pond, and pine woodlands and provides viewing for wading and waterbirds, native and migrant passerine birds, and marsh-dwelling reptiles, amphibians, and mammals. Mackay Island Road and dike trails are open spring through fall for foot and bicycle travel, and offer prime viewing of wading and waterbirds, especially in the East Pool and around Live Oak Point; also wetland-dwelling mammals, reptiles, and amphibians. Canals allow good wildlife watching from a canoe or small boat.

Directions: Reached from Virginia by NC 615 and from Currituck mainland by free public ferry. Refuge headquarters on NC 615 near community of Knotts Island.

Ownership: USFWS (919-429-3100)   **Size:** 7,800 acres

Closest Town: Village of Knotts Island

The osprey, also known as the fish hawk, is often seen hovering above streams, lakes, and coastal waters as it searches for unsuspecting fish.
KEN TAYLOR

33

Coastal Plain

The state's eastern half is composed of sedimentary rocks and soil deposited over the ages by rivers and the sea. Rivers flow eastward into sounds as wide and shallow estuaries. Some rivers originating in the piedmont region carry large loads of sediments and are known as "brownwater" rivers; other rivers draining from swamps carry dark organic material, giving them the descriptive name "blackwater" rivers.

The region's uplands were once covered by ten million acres of longleaf pine and hardwood forests, but both ecosystems are now greatly reduced. The pine forests were dependent upon frequent wildfires, with native plant and animal species adapted to fire. Forest managers nowadays must recreate this natural process in preserved areas. Much of the region was once covered by swamp forests of bald cypress, gum, and white cedar trees, as well as shrub bogs. The bogs flourished in peat deposits known by the Indian word "pocosins." Half of the state's wetlands have been destroyed since the arrival of European settlers; many wetlands were drained and converted to farming and industrial timber production.

Along the region's estuaries and sounds are great expanses of freshwater or brackish marshes. The southern coastal plain is marked by thousands of elliptical depressions called "Carolina bays." These unique formations are geologic mysteries, as no one is quite sure how they were formed. The interior southern coastal area harbors the Sandhills region, one million acres of sandy soil that once supported longleaf pine forests and grasslands. Natural areas in the coastal plain support a wide variety of wildlife, with many animals found only in specialized habitats.

Cypress Swamp, Greenfield Lake KEN TAYLOR

SITE NUMBER	SITE NAME
20	Alligator River National Wildlife Refuge
21	Dismal Swamp National Wildlife Refuge
22	Merchants Millpond State Park
23	Roanoke River Bottomlands
24	Pettigrew State Park and Lake Phelps
25	Pocosin Lakes National Wildlife Refuge
26	Lake Mattamuskeet National Wildlife Refuge
27	Gull Rock Game Land
28	Swan Quater National Wildlife Refuge
29	Goose Creek State Park
30	Goose Creek Game Land

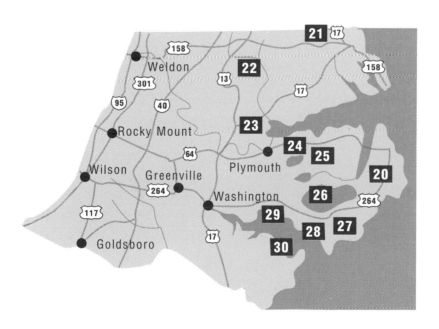

20 | Alligator River National Wildlife Refuge

Description: Nearly extinct just a decade ago, red wolves again roam this expanse of wildlands following a successful reintroduction program. Refuge features full spectrum of wetland habitats associated with peatlands. One of the region's largest black bear populations found here, as well as otter, deer, and marsh rabbit. Rare species inhabiting the refuge include red-cockaded woodpecker, bald eagle, and alligator. Many warblers, woodpeckers, hawks, owls, and other woodland bird species are residents; large numbers of geese, swans, and diving ducks winter along the river and in flooded fields. The U.S. Air Force bombing range, located within refuge boundaries, provides an additional 45,000 acres of wildlife habitat.

Viewing Information: No improved facilities. Dirt roads lead from U.S. 64 and U.S. 264 into the heart of the refuge. The Buffalo City road runs south from U.S. 64 to a boat ramp on Milltail Creek, a scenic blackwater stream. BE AWARE OF HAZARDOUS CONDITIONS ON OLD LOGGING ROADS; OFF-ROAD VEHICLES ADVISED. Visitors will not see the secretive red wolf.

Directions: U.S. 264 traverses refuge's southern and eastern sections, with good views of wetland habitats. U.S. 64 passes through the northern sector, with unpaved side roads into refuge.

Ownership: USFWS (919-473-1131)

Size: Approximately 150,000 acres   **Closest Town:** Manns Harbor

Like most wading birds, great blue herons depend on high water quality and rich wetland habitats. KEITH LONGIOTTI

Nearly extinct in the wild a decade ago, red wolves have been returned to their natural range in the Alligator River wilderness and the Smoky Mountains.
GRADY ALLEN

21 | Dismal Swamp National Wildlife Refuge

Description: Reduced in size, altered ecologically, Great Dismal Swamp National Wildlife Refuge nonetheless retains one of the largest protected areas of swamp wilderness in the eastern U.S. Younger, second-growth trees have replaced the original cypress, gum, and Atlantic white cedar forest. Swamp provides habitat for a wide variety of birds, reptiles, and amphibians; also mammals, including black bear, otter, bobcat, mink, foxes, bats, and deer. Known for large numbers of woodland bird species, including Swainson's and prothonotory warblers, owls, and woodpeckers. Haven for migratory warblers, thrushes, and other landbirds. Massive flocks of robins and blackbirds winter in swamp. Watch for red-bellied sliders and chicken turtles. Refuge management programs attempt to restore and maintain natural biological diversity.

Viewing Information: Refuge straddles N.C.-Virgina border; access roads and interpretive facilities are in Virginia. Refuge is open all year. Visitors should stay on designated trails. SWAMP IN SUMMER IS HOT AND INSECT RIDDEN. Most comfortable times to visit in fall and spring. More than 210 species of birds, including thirty-four warbler species, observed here. Bird watching is best during spring migration from April to June.

Directions: Refuge headquarters and main access points in Virginia reached from Suffolk south on U.S. 13 and VA 32 about 4.5 miles, then follow signs. To reach Dismal Town Boardwalk Trail, take White Marsh Road (VA 642) to Washington Ditch refuge entrance. Small boat access to 3,000-acre Lake Drummond by feeder ditch from U.S. 17 and Intercoastal Waterway on east side of refuge. U.S. 158 skirts southern border of refuge.

Ownership: USFWS (804-986-3705)

Size: 24,812 acres in NC and 82,059 acres in VA

Closest Towns: Sunbury and South Mills in NC, Suffolk in VA

The prothonotary warbler is among forty species of warblers native to North Carolina. The tiny bird favors deep woods and swamp forests, and may be seen along streams.
PARIS TRAIL

Description: This 760-acre pond created 180 years ago on Bennetts Creek is a flooded forest of large bald cypress and tupelo gum, including a grove of huge, old-growth cypress. Wildlife include river otter, mink, muskrat, deer, gray fox, occasional black bear and bobcat, and reintroduced beaver. One beaver dam stretches 2,100 feet. Watch for turtles, frogs, and snakes basking on logs and stumps. Hundreds of ducks winter on the pond; 160 species of birds observed in the park. Warblers, waterbirds, owls, and woodpeckers are plentiful. Bennetts Creek flows from millpond to Chowan River swamp.

Viewing Information: Popular for canoeing; rental canoes available at park. Trails with foot bridges loop nearly seven miles along shoreline, through swamps and upland forest.

Directions: Millpond access from U.S. 158 and 1.5 miles south on SR 1403, 4.3 miles east of Gatesville; park office and campground located .5 mile east of U.S. 158 and SR 1403 crossroads.

Additional Viewing Opportunities: Chowan River Swamp and Game Lands.

Ownership: NCDPR (919-357-1191)   **Size:** 2,918 acres

Closest Towns: Gatesville and Sunbury

Description: Old-growth bottomland forests here teem with wildlife, including river otter, beaver, bobcat, mink, gray fox, gray squirrel, and marsh rabbit. Wild turkey, cerulean warbler, and Mississippi kite are among 220 breeding bird species. Bald eagles occasionally seen. Large flocks of wintering puddle ducks, such as mallards, black ducks and wood ducks, use the backswamps for feeding and roosting. Site of state's largest inland nesting colonies of great blue herons and great egrets.

Viewing Information: Public access primarily by boat, with exception of pullouts on U.S. 17 for Conine Island tract, north of Williamston. Public boat ramps are located in or near closest towns listed below. Hunting occurs in fall and winter. Contact administrative offices for current regulations.

Directions: River crossings in middle section of river on U.S. 258 and NC 11, and downstream on U.S. 17 at Williamston and NC 45 near river mouth below Plymouth.

Ownership: USFWS (919-794-5326), NCWRC (919-733-7291), TNC (919-967-7007)

Size: 49,000 acres planned for protection

Closest Towns: Plymouth, Williamston, Roanoke Rapids

24 Pettigrew State Park and Lake Phelps

Description: Lake Phelps is second-largest natural lake in the state. Shoreline areas vegetated by freshwater marsh, pond pine pocosin, and mature cypress swamp. Lake is a winter resting area for waterfowl, including tundra swans, Canada geese, and numerous species of dabbling and diving ducks. Wood duck and a few hooded mergansers, mallards, and black ducks remain year-round to nest. View a variety of herons, egrets, spotted sandpipers, and birds of prey, including occasional bald eagles. Forty species of breeding birds have been observed, including Louisiana waterthrush. Shoreline wetlands are habitat for many snakes and turtles.

Viewing Information: More than four miles of park hiking trails along northern lake shore begin near park information center. Boat launch and pier near park office. A 300-foot boardwalk through swamp forest is ideal for viewing wildlife. Park adjacent to Somerset Place Plantation Historic Site.

Directions: South off U.S. 64 at Creswell, following park signs for seven miles on SR 1142, 1160 and 1168 to entry gate.

Ownership: NCDPR (919-797-4475)

Size: 16,600 acres of lake and 1,143 acres of land   **Closest Town:** Creswell

25 Pocosin Lakes National Wildlife Refuge

Description: New refuge encompassing older Pungo wildlife refuge. Winter resting area for several thousand tundra swans, Canada geese, and duck species. Raptors occasionally seen. Black bears and other mammals inhabit the area. Refuge lands encompass Lake Pungo, New Lake, and tracts on the Scuppernong River, and provides important wildlife corridors linking with the Alligator River and Lake Mattamuskeet refuges. A beautiful blackwater stream, the Scuppernong River meanders out of the peatlands to Bulls Bay on the Albemarle Sound. The river is bordered by extensive stands of Atlantic white cedar and swamp forests inhabited by abundant wildlife.

Viewing Information: Facilities under development; existing access and foot trails for Pungo Lake. Scuppernong River is popular for wildlife viewing from small boats and canoes.

Directions: Pungo Lake east of NC 99/45 via SR 1338 on western side of refuge; NC 94 bisects eastern section of refuge. A public boat ramp is located on the Scuppernong River in the town of Columbia.

Ownership: USFWS (919-797-4431), TNC on Scuppernong River (919- 967-7007)

Size: 111,000 acres   **Closest Towns:** Creswell, Columbia

Description: Indian legends told of a gigantic wildfire in prehistoric times that burned through organic soils, leaving a basin that later filled with water and formed Lake Mattamuskeet, the largest natural lake in North Carolina. Abundant aquatic foods and surrounding croplands create ideal habitat for many thousands of wintering tundra swans, snow geese, Canada geese, and ducks. Half of all the tundra swans on the Atlantic Flyway winter here—some 45,000 birds. Hawks, bald eagles and occasional golden eagles also seen in winter. Large numbers of migratory shorebirds like dowitchers and sandpipers feed along lakeshore. Lake sustains one of state's largest breeding populations of osprey. Canals are good places to see otter. Deer easily observed in woods.

Viewing Information: Refuge open daylight hours only. View birds from pullovers off NC 94 causeway, along entrance road; other access roads north from U.S. 264. November through February best time to see migratory waterfowl and raptors.

Directions: North of U.S. 264; refuge divided by NC 94 causeway. Refuge headquarters on southern shore near historic lodge and pump station.

Ownership: USFWS (919-926-4021)

Size: 50,000 acres **Closest Town:** Fairfield

P 🛶 🚤

The U.S. Fish and Wildlife Service provides wildlife viewing stations in many refuges, including this observation stand at Lake Pungo in the Pocosin Lakes refuge. Wintering waterfowl are a major viewing attraction here. KEN TAYLOR/N.C. WILDLIFE

27 Gull Rock Game Land

Description: Excellent wetland habitats, including brackish marshes, low and high pocosin bogs, bald cypress stands, pond pine woodlands, and hardwood forested flats. More than sixty species of breeding birds observed. Waterfowl concentrations in impoundments and marshes near the sound. Deer, raccoons, and otter most frequently seen mammals. Small population of alligators and many black bears present. Located just east of the Swan Quarter wildlife refuge and south of Lake Mattamuskeet refuge

Viewing Information: Best times to vist the game lands are on non-hunting days. HUNTING OCCURS DURING FALL, WINTER, AND APRIL—MAY ON MONDAYS THROUGH SATURDAYS AND HOLIDAYS. Side roads for off-road vehicles and hikers reached from access roads. Side road gates closed March 1 through August 31. Launch ramps for private boats.

Directions: Access south from U.S. 264 via SR 1122 or 1164.

Ownership: NCWRC (919-733-7291)

Size: 12,000 acres   **Closest Town:** New Holland

28 Swan Quarter National Wildlife Refuge

Description: Great expanses of black needlerush and other marsh grasses dominate this brackish marsh ecosystem bordering Pamlico Sound. Refuge contains marsh islands, tidal creeks, and swamp forests. Tens of thousands of canvasback, scaup, bufflehead, redhead, and ruddy ducks and other waterfowl winter in adjacent bays. Osprey and other raptors, herons, and egrets frequently seen. Small population of alligator.

Viewing Information: Marked access road into refuge from U.S. 264, west of the town of Swan Quarter, leads to a 1,100-foot wooden pier on Rose Bay. Refuge best explored by boat. Refuge open only during daylight hours. Excellent way to see wintering waterfowl is from Ocracoke-Swan Quarter public ferry.

Directions: East from Washington, NC, and southwest of Lake Mattamuskeet, on the south side of U.S. 264; Rose Bay access road marked from U.S. 264; state ferry landing and private boat ramp south of the town of Swan Quarter via NC 45 and SR 1132.

Ownership: USFWS (919-926-4021)

Size: 15,500 acres   **Closest Town:** Swan Quarter

Description: Borders Pamlico River and Goose Creek tributary. Brackish and freshwater marshes, swamp forests, and upland pine woodlands support abundant wildlife in a scenic setting. Marshes here are excellent examples of low-salinity wetlands. Area serves as nursery for many fish and other marine animals. Diving ducks inhabit the sound and creeks, especially during winter. Marshes support rails, marsh wrens, herons, and egrets; also wood ducks, pileated and red-cockaded woodpeckers, hawks, and many warblers and vireos. River otter, marsh rabbits, mink, raccoons, muskrats, gray fox, elusive bobcat, abundant white-tailed deer.

Viewing Information: Nearly seven miles of well-marked trails wind through park. Trailheads lead from parking lots. The Flatty Creek Trail includes a short boardwalk and observation deck to view the beautiful creek and marshlands.

Directions: On north side of Pamlico River; from Washington, NC, follow U.S. 264 for ten miles, turn onto SR 1334 for 2.5 miles to park entrance.

Ownership: NCDPR (919-923-2191)

Size: 1,596 acres **Closest Town:** Bath

The scenic live oak trail in Goose Creek State Park follows the shore of the Pamlico River. More than 2,400 miles of hiking trails are found in North Carolina.
WALTER C. BIGGS

30 Goose Creek Game Land

Description: A series of four impoundments, each about 200 acres in size, on a peninsula along the south side of the Pamlico River. The wildlife management areas maintain shallow pools of freshwater surrounded by marshes. Impoundments support large numbers of wintering and migrating waterfowl, also shorebirds. Common breeding birds are pied-billed grebe, least bittern, black duck, blue-winged teal, seaside sparrows, black rail, and others. Many egrets and herons feed here; large numbers of shorebirds. Nearby Gum Swamp contains a large tract of old-growth cypress swamp and pocosins, important habitat for wildlife such as black bear, deer, otter, nutria, muskrat, fox, bobcat, and other small mammals.

Viewing Information: Boat access required to see much of the area. Water can be rough; boats sixteen feet or larger advised. Best times to visit the game lands are on non-hunting days. HUNTING OCCURS DURING FALL, WINTER, AND APRIL-MAY ON MONDAYS, WEDNESDAYS, SATURDAYS AND HOLIDAYS. Gates closed March 1-August 31. Best time to observe waterfowl in February-March; best time to see wading birds from May to August.

Directions: Impoundments are north and east of NC 33 and are best reached by boat from several public launch sites. Swamp forest is south and west of NC 33.

Ownership: NCWRC (919-733-7291 or 638-3000)

Size: 7,600 acres   **Closest Town:** Hobucken

Great numbers of snow geese may be seen during the winter at Lake Mattamuskeet and other coastal plain sites. KEN TAYLOR

SITE
NUMBER

SITE
NAME

31   **Cedar Island National Wildlife Refuge**
32   **Croatan Pocosin Wilderness Areas and Lakes**
33   **Millis Road Savanna**
34   **Patsy Pond**
35   **Cedar Point—White Oak River**
36   **Cliffs of the Neuse River State Park**
37   **Holly Shelter Game Land**
38   **Black River**
39   **Waccamaw Lake and River**
40   **Lumber River**
41   **Bladen Lakes Educational State Forest**
42   **Jones Lake State Park**
43   **Fort Bragg Army Installation**
44   **Sandhills Game Land**
45   **Weymounth Woods Preserve**

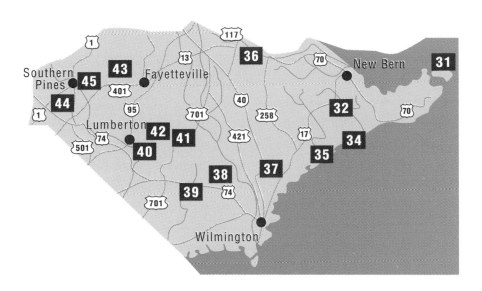

31 Cedar Island National Wildlife Refuge

Description: Vast marshes on peninsula stretch six miles on both sides of NC 12. Habitat for black rail and other more common rails, along with marsh and sedge wrens, seaside sparrows, great horned and barred owls. In winter see northern harriers, occasional merlin, bald eagle, or peregrine falcon. Ferry terminal from Cedar Island to Ocracoke provides excellent viewing of swallows, migrant landbirds, raptors, waterfowl, skimmers, sandpipers, and pelicans.

Viewing Information: Best observation sites from road shoulders along NC 12, at refuge office area, and ferry terminal. Refuge open daylight hours only. Best viewing for migratory birds in fall and winter.

Directions: Take U.S. 70 and NC 12 east forty-five miles from Morehead City-Beaufort to Cedar Island ferry terminal at northeastern end of island for passage to Ocracoke Island across the Pamlico Sound.

Ownership: USFWS (919-225-2511)

Size: 14,482 acres   **Closest Towns:** Cedar Island and Atlantic

P ⛺ 🚣 🛥️ 🚤

32 Croatan Pocosin Wilderness Areas and Lakes

Description: Croatan National Forest contains some of the largest and best examples of "pocosins"—freshwater wetlands formed on deep peat deposits, vegetated by evergreen shrubs, dwarfed pond pine, and bay trees. These ecosystems are adapted to occasional wildfires. Four tracts designated national wilderness areas. Within the pocosin bogs are scattered lakes, which may have been formed by massive fires that burned through the peat to create water-filled basins. Among them are Catfish and Great Lakes. Wetland habitats support black bear, alligator and other reptiles, numerous warblers, and other birds.

Viewing Information: Wetlands areas not easily accessible, but visitors can drive between the pocosin wilderness areas from U.S. 70 to NC 58 on SR 1100 and SR 1105, and drive to boat ramps and viewing sites on Catfish Lake and Great Lake roads. OFF-ROAD VEHICLES RECOMMENDED FOR ROAD TO GREAT LAKE.

Directions: Contact USFS for national forest map showing public access roads and viewing sites.

Ownership: USFS (919-638-5628)

Size: 35,000 acres   **Closest Town:** Havelock

P 🚣 🛥️

One of nature's oldest living creatures, American alligators may be seen basking on lake shores, in marshes, and streams. Alligators do most of their hunting at night and will eat fish, birds, and small mammals. KEITH LONGIOTTI

33 | Millis Road Savanna

Description: This longleaf pine savanna in the Croatan National Forest is one of the state's best. A variety of wildflowers found here, along with many rare plant species. Colonies of endangered red-cockaded woodpeckers nest in mature pines, distinguished by the white shine of running sap. Rare Bachman's sparrow nests in wiregrass; Henslow's sparrow found in winter. Also see pine warbler, bluebird, chickadees, flicker, downy and hairy woodpeckers, catbird, yellowthroat, and other resident birds. Savanna ecosystem dependent upon periodic fires that maintain open condition.

Viewing Information: Designated natural area on south side of Millis Road. Park on the roadside shoulder; avoid deep sand. Consult national forest map.

Directions: North from NC 24 for about three miles on SR 1124 (Nine Foot Road); turn left onto unpaved SR 1112 (Forest Service road 128 Millis Road); go about 1.5 miles—savanna is on south side of the road. Park on road shoulder but avoid deep sands. USE CAUTION IN DRIVING ON SAND ROADS; AVOID IN WET WEATHER.

Ownership: USFS (919-638-5628) **Size:** 300 acres **Closest Town:** Newport

34 | Patsy Pond

Description: A series of natural ponds in the swales among ancient beach ridges support unusual plants and are especially scenic. The dry sand ridges and flats between the ponds are forested by longleaf pine and turkey oak with heath shrubs. A colony of endangered red-cockaded woodpeckers may be found near the ponds. Rare Bachman's sparrows also nest here. Carolina gopher frog and other reptiles and amphibians abundant in pond margins. Watch for many kinds of dragonflies.

Viewing Information: Foot trails lead from Pringle Road (Forest Service Road 123) and loop around the ponds.

Directions: Turn north from NC 24 about six miles east from Cape Carteret and two miles east of town of Ocean; park on roadside access along Pringle Road (sand base road on west side of the ponds) and follow foot trails.

Ownership: USFS (919-638-5628) **Size:** 70 acres **Closest Town:** Ocean

No camouflage here. This tiny red eft is a blaze of color on its bed of moss. KEN TAYLOR

35 Cedar Point—White Oak River

Description: Salt and brackish marshes and tidal creeks found near the mouth of the White Oak River are typical of coastal estuarine systems. The marshes provide habitat for many birds, mammals, fish, and other aquatic life. Birds seen here include terns and gulls, herons, egrets, and osprey. Upland slopes feature woodlands with maritime forest characteristics.

Viewing Information: One-mile, self-guided "Cedar Point Tideland" foot trail and boardwalks loop from the riverside parking lot. Observation decks and blinds located along the path. River popular for boating and fishing.

Directions: Access marked to Cedar Point recreation area from NC 58, to end of SR 1114 on the shore of the White Oak River. Turn west from NC 58 onto SR 1114 and travel about one mile north from Cape Carteret.

Ownership: USFS (919-638-5628)

Size: 260 acres

Closest Towns: Cape Carteret and Swansboro

36 Cliffs of the Neuse River State Park

Description: Sedimentary cliffs tower ninety feet over the Neuse River and its forested floodplain. Exposed layers of sand, gravel, limestone, and fossils found here. Forest habitats are representative of the region and support diverse wildlife. Breeding birds include the northern parula nesting in clumps of Spanish moss, and prothonotary warbler in riverside swamp forests. Pileated woodpecker resides here with other woodpecker species. Wood ducks nest near the river in hollow trees. Hawks and bald eagles often seen. Resident mammals include white-tailed deer, raccoon, foxes, opossum, and gray squirrels, and muskrat or river otter. Reptiles such as skinks, Carolina anoles, turtles, and snakes may be seen throughout the park, along with many amphibians.

Viewing Information: Several park trails originate near the interpretive museum, which contains exhibits about the park's geologic, natural, and cultural history. Paths with rail fences lead along the cliff edge to an observation deck.

Directions: Along the Neuse River fourteen miles southeast of Goldsboro on NC 111; access road is SR 1743 on east side of NC 111.

Ownership: NCDPR (919-778-6234)

Size: 750 acres

Closest Town: Seven Springs (on NC 55)

37 | Holly Shelter Game Land

Description: A great wilderness of pocosin and swamp wetlands, interspersed by forested sand ridges. Full range of Coastal Plain habitats found here. Secluded region provides habitat for many animals including black bear and alligator. Colonies of endangered red-cockaded woodpecker inhabit ridgetop pine savannas. Songbirds are abundant, along with woodpeckers, bobwhite quail, and raptors. Bald eagles sometimes seen. View wood ducks, mallards, and other waterfowl. Mammals include deer, fox, bobcat, gray squirrels, and fox squirrels. In wetland areas look for insect-eating plants such as Venus flytrap, pitcherplants, and sundews.

Viewing Information: Best times to visit the game lands are on non-hunting days. HUNTING OCCURS DURING FALL, WINTER, AND APRIL-MAY ON MONDAYS, WEDNESDAYS, SATURDAYS, AND HOLIDAYS. Visitors may park on road shoulders and follow foot trails. Gates are locked March 1- August 31, requiring a longer walk into site. Contact office for more information.

Directions: East of the Northeast Cape Fear River and south of NC 53 via SR 1520; or northwest of U.S. 17 via Lodge Road. Sand roads bisect game land. Public boat ramp on Northeast Cape Fear River near the western gate.

Ownership: NCWRC (919-259-5555 or 733-7291)

Size: 48,795 acres   **Closest Town:** Hampstead

38 | Black River

Description: Some of the bald cypress trees in this magnificent swamp forest are known to be 1,600 years old—the oldest living trees in eastern North America. Forest includes cypress, gum, red maple, and overcup oak. Watch for river otter, prothonotary and other warblers, pileated and other woodpeckers, turtles, and snakes.

Viewing Information: Access only by small boat or canoe; portions of cypress forest visible from bridge crossings. SHORELINE PRIVATELY OWNED; DO NOT TRESPASS.

Directions: Bridge crossings by SR 1201-1550 and NC 53-11; public boat ramp on south side of river below NC 53 crossing.

Additional Viewing Opportunities: Nearby on NC 210 is Moores Creek National Battlefield, a Revolutionary War historic site and area of botanical interest.

Ownership: TNC (919-967-7007) and PVT

Size: 2,600 acres   **Closest Town:** Atkinson

Description: Largest of the Carolina bay lakes. Features extraordinary aquatic life; numerous small fish and mollusks are found nowhere else in the world. Moderate numbers of waterfowl may be seen. A swamp forest borders southern lake shore. The Waccamaw River flows southward from the lake. Along river, view many warblers and other songbirds, wading birds, hawks and owls, occasional alligator, many water snakes, turtles, black bear, white-tailed deer, river otter, and smaller mammals.

Viewing Information: In the state park, walking trails and boardwalks follow the lake shore; a long pier extends out into the lake. Public boat ramps. River is best seen from small boat or canoe.

Directions: Twelve miles east of Whiteville and thirty-eight miles west of Wilmington. South from U.S. 74 at town of Lake Waccamaw; follow state park signs to park entrance on southeast side of lake. River is reached at its lake source by SR 1967 west of the park, or downstream from bridge crossings by SR 1928 or NC 130 and 904.

Additional Viewing Opportunities: The Green Swamp Preserve, owned by The Nature Conservancy, is located to the east and open to guided tours by reservation. Call TNC at 919-967-7007.

Ownership: NCDPR (919-669-2928) and PVT

Size: lake 8,938 acres; park 1,732 acres; river swamp approximately 20,000 acres

Closest Town: Lake Waccamaw

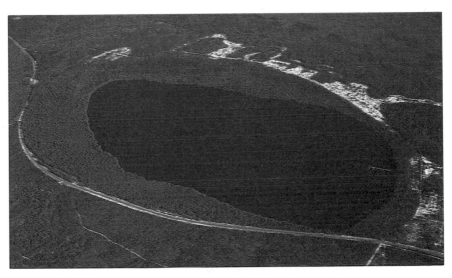

Carolina bays are geologic mysteries: no one is quite sure how they were formed. The state's coastal plain is dotted with these oval basins, some filled with water, others vegetated by wetland plants. KEN TAYLOR/N.C. WILDLIFE

40 Lumber River

Description: Local Indians knew it as the "Lumbee", their tribal name, but settlers renamed it "Lumber" for the amount of timber rafted downstream to sawmills. This beautiful blackwater stream meanders through swamp forests for 102 miles before reaching South Carolina. The designated State Natural and Scenic River carries boaters past bottomland forests that harbor abundant wildlife. Wildlife commonly seen along the river include beaver, otter, deer, waterfowl, and many other species of birds. Also known for high diversity of reptiles and amphibians.

Viewing Information: Best seen by small boat or canoe launched from any of several bridge crossings. The river segment above Lumberton designated as "scenic" and below Lumberton as "natural." Land for state park facilities is currently being acquired below Lumberton, including the "Net Hole" area of extension floodplain swamp forest.

Directions: Numerous road crossings and access points to the river. SR 1412 in Scotland County crosses at head of the river; also Wildlife Resources landing at the NC 72 crossing south of Lumberton, and U.S. 74 or NC 904 bridges farther downstream.

Ownership: NCDPR (919-733-4181) and PVT   **Size:** 102 miles of river

Closest Towns: Maxton, Lumberton, Fair Bluff

River otters are widespread in coastal rivers, streams, and estuaries, but rarely seen in the rest of the state. One of nature's most playful animals, the river otter will build a mudslide on a steep river bank and pass the time careening into the water. JAMES F. PARNELL

41 Bladen Lakes Educational State Forest

Description: "Educational forest" is 1,200-acre section of a much larger managed forest. Along with pine plantations, site contains tracts of seven intact natural habitats, ranging from pine woodlands to pocosin shrub bogs with masses of pitcher plants. This variety of habitats harbors a wide spectrum of wildlife from black bear to more common species of mammals, reptiles and amphibians. View colonies of endangered red-cockaded woodpecker and uncommon pine barrens treefrog. Fox squirrels and a rich variety of birdlife found here.

Viewing Information: Self-guided auto tour route east from NC 242 with interpretive stops for Turnbull Creek Trail, Post Trail, Pine Straw Trail, Fire Control Trail, and "Talking Tree" exhibit. Hunting not permitted within educational forest.

Directions: From Elizabethtown, go four miles north on NC 242. About .5 mile north of the entrance to Jones Lake State Park, turn east onto SR 1511; go .5 mile to educational forest entrance on right.

Ownership: NCDFR (919-588-4161)

Size: 1,200 acres designated as educational forest within 35,000 acre state forest

Closest Town: Elizabethtown

42 Jones Lake State Park

Description: Park features Jones and Salters lakes, both outstanding examples of unique Carolina bays. Lake waters are dark-colored, highly acidic, and low in nutrients. A variety of turtles and water snakes may be seen along the shoreline swamp and bay forests. Occasional flocks of ducks rest here; wood ducks nest in area. Surrounding bay forest supports warblers and bobcat, black bear, white-tailed deer, gray and fox squirrels. Colonies of endangered red-cockaded woodpeckers in pine forests; look for nesting trees, clearly identified by white resin dripping from the cavities. Pinewoods treefrogs and carpenter frogs heard singing in summer months.

Viewing Information: Self-guided three-mile trail around Jones Lake, leading from swimming beach and campground; park rangers will give access instructions for reaching Salters Lake natural area.

Directions: Four miles north of Elizabethtown on west side of NC 242.

Additional Viewing Opportunities: Nearby is Bushy Lake state natural area; contact Jones Lake park rangers for more information.

Ownership: NCDPR (919-588-4550)

Size: 1,669 acres   **Closest Town:** Elizabethtown

43 Fort Bragg Army Installation

Description: Gently rolling terrain dominated by huge expanses of longleaf pine and turkey oak forests with wiregrass ground cover. The endangered red-cockaded woodpecker is featured viewing species here, with over 400 colonies throughout the installation. Also excellent place to view bluebirds along twenty-five-mile bluebird trail. Rare Bachman's sparrow nests in grasses under pines. White-tailed deer, fox squirrel, and numerous raptors may also be observed here. Abundant wildflowers and butterflies.

Viewing Information: RED-COCKADED WOODPECKER IS ENDANGERED SPECIES; DO NOT HARASS OR HANDLE IN ANY WAY. Best viewing for woodpeckers in the spring during early morning and late evening. Look for woodpeckers' cavity trees, distinguished by white resin sap and by painted bands and markers. DEEP SAND; USE CAUTION WHEN PULLING ONTO ROADSIDES. CERTAIN AREAS OF THE INSTALLATION ARE OFF LIMITS; ALL VISITORS MUST REPORT TO THE HUNTING AND FISHING CENTER BEFORE PROCEEDING THROUGH INSTALLATION.

Directions: From Fayetteville follow U.S. 24 west to Butner Road entrance to Fort Bragg. Proceed west on Butner Road approximately three miles to Gruber Road. Turn north onto Gruber Road and travel one mile to the Hunting and Fishing Center. Designated viewing area located near the center.

Ownership: US Army (919-432-5325)

Size: 150,000 acres   **Closest Town:** Fayetteville

P🏕🏛🍴

Loss of habitat has created an uncertain future for the endangered red-cockaded woodpecker. The birds nest in colonies in old-growth pine forests, which are growing scarce in North Carolina.
KEN TAYLOR

44 | Sandhills Game Land

Description: Largest natural reserve in the Sandhills region. Habitats include old-growth longleaf pine flatwoods and savannas, Atlantic white cedar stands, bay heads with pond pine and evergreen shrubs, hardwood swamps, blackwater streams, and bluffs covered by mountain laurel. These diverse communities and extreme wet and dry conditions provide habitat for many animals, also numerous rare plants. Many amphibians and reptiles here, including scarlet king snake, northern pine snake, and pygmy rattler. Spectacular springtime choruses of frogs, including pine barrens treefrog. Rare Bachman's sparrow nests in grasses; colonies of endangered red-cockaded woodpecker found in mature pine stands. Watch for fox squirrels, white-tail deer, red and grey foxes, as well as many butterflies native to this ecosystem.

Viewing Information: Bisected by public roads; visitors advised to stop at the headquarters located on the west side of U.S. 1 south of Hoffman for viewing advice. Best times to visit the game lands are on non-hunting days. HUNTING OCCURS DURING FALL, WINTER, AND APRIL-MAY ON MONDAYS, WEDNESDAYS, SATURDAYS, AND HOLIDAYS. USE CAUTION PARKING ON ROAD SHOULDERS; AVOID DEEP SAND.

Directions: West and east sides of U.S. 1, ten miles north of Rockingham or fifteen miles south of Southern Pines.

Ownership: NCWRC (919-733-7291 or 281-3917)

Size: 57,250 acres   **Closest Town:** Hoffman

45 | Weymouth Woods Preserve

Description: Prominent habitats are savannas of longleaf pine and turkey oak on sand ridges, bottomland hardwoods, and small streams and bogs. On a separate tract is a stand of 200-400 year old longleaf pine and mature black oaks. In the preserve is a colony of endangered red-cockaded woodpeckers, along with 260 other bird species. Commonly seen wildlife includes salamanders, snakes, skinks, box turtles, and many frogs and toads, including the uncommon pine barrens treefrog. Watch for fox squirrels in longleaf pine forest.

Viewing Information: Self-guided loop trails from interpretive center and museum located on the south side of the preserve. Interpretive programs and natural history exhibits.

Directions: One mile southeast of Southern Pines, east from U.S. 1 on Ft. Bragg Road (SR 2074).

Ownership: NCDPR (919-692-2167)

Size: 676 acres   **Closest Town:** Southern Pines and Aberdeen

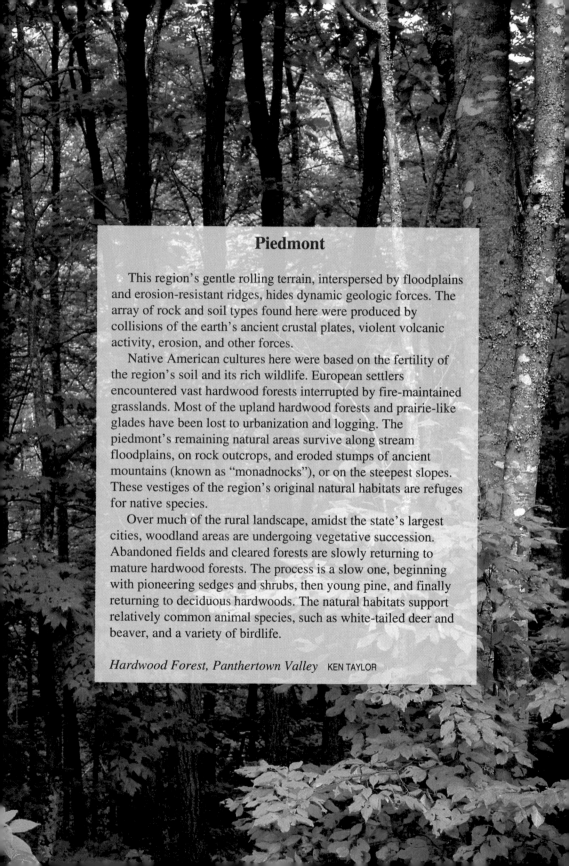

Piedmont

This region's gentle rolling terrain, interspersed by floodplains and erosion-resistant ridges, hides dynamic geologic forces. The array of rock and soil types found here were produced by collisions of the earth's ancient crustal plates, violent volcanic activity, erosion, and other forces.

Native American cultures here were based on the fertility of the region's soil and its rich wildlife. European settlers encountered vast hardwood forests interrupted by fire-maintained grasslands. Most of the upland hardwood forests and prairie-like glades have been lost to urbanization and logging. The piedmont's remaining natural areas survive along stream floodplains, on rock outcrops, and eroded stumps of ancient mountains (known as "monadnocks"), or on the steepest slopes. These vestiges of the region's original natural habitats are refuges for native species.

Over much of the rural landscape, amidst the state's largest cities, woodland areas are undergoing vegetative succession. Abandoned fields and cleared forests are slowly returning to mature hardwood forests. The process is a slow one, beginning with pioneering sedges and shrubs, then young pine, and finally returning to deciduous hardwoods. The natural habitats support relatively common animal species, such as white-tailed deer and beaver, and a variety of birdlife.

Hardwood Forest, Panthertown Valley KEN TAYLOR

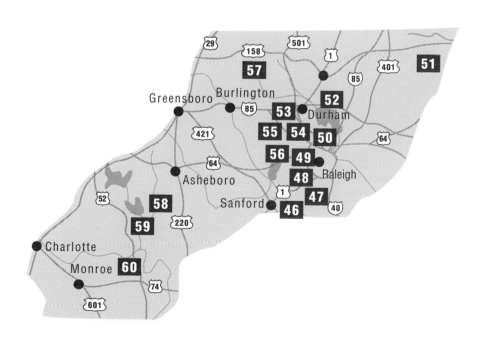

46 Raven Rock State Park

Description: The bluffs here tower 150 feet over Cape Fear River. This area is the "fall line" where piedmont and coastal plain regions merge. Forests typical of mature and successional habitats of eastern piedmont, with pines and hardwoods on bluff tops and alluvial hardwoods covering slopes and floodplain. Many springs and streams. Interesting rock outcrops. Diversity of wildflowers. Abundant wildlife especially noted for rich bird life, amphibians, and mammals, including southern flying squirrel, fox squirrel, and bats. River courses through moderate rapids and ancient Indian "fish trap" rock dams.

Viewing Information: Variety of foot and bridle trails throughout park; canoeing on river with canoe camping; cliffside wooden stairs and overlook on Raven Rock trail.

Directions: Nine miles west of Lillington and twenty miles east of Sanford; from Lillington turn west from U.S. 421 and follow SR 1314 three miles to park entrance.

Ownership: NCDPR (919-893-4888)

Size: 2,990 acres   **Closest Town:** Lillington

47 Harris Lake

Description: Large power plant reservoir surrounded by successional pine, mixed hardwood forests, and abandoned fields typical of eastern piedmont region. Common wildlife include woodland and field birds, small mammals, white-tailed deer, reptiles, and amphibians. Reservoir and bottomland forests of nearby Cape Fear River provide habitat for osprey, bald eagles, waterfowl, and wading birds. Species tallies of twenty-six mammals, 156 birds, thirty-three reptiles, and twenty-two amphibians. Reservoir popular for recreational fishing with seventy-two fish species.

Viewing Information: Site offers year-round viewing opportunities. Harris Visitors Center has reservoir and site maps, also species lists. Best viewing locations include Harris Lake, wildlife refuge and management areas, and White Oak Nature Trail, which loops from picnic area at the Harris Visitors Center.

Directions: Exit U.S. 1 at New Hill (eight miles southwest of Apex or twenty-two miles northeast of Sanford); then drive 1.5 miles south on SR 1127 to Harris Visitors Center at the the Harris Energy & Environmental Center.

Ownership: Carolina Power & Light Co. (Harris Visitors Center 919-362-3261)

Size: 11,700 acres   **Closest Town:** New Hill

Description: Site features Canadian hemlock trees at southeastern limit of range, atop dramatic eighty-foot bluffs. Along with mountain-type plants on cool north slopes are more representative eastern piedmont upland and bottomland hardwood and pine forests. High wildflower diversity on bluffs. Good spot to view variety of woodland birds. Shallow ponds on Swift Creek's floodplain support many reptiles and amphibians including spotted, marbled, red-backed and other salamanders. Upstream from Swift Creek Bluffs nature preserve.

Viewing Information: Self-guided foot trails with boardwalks through wet floodplain; wooden steps and observation decks on bluff tops. Nature center under development.

Directions: *South of Cary and U.S. 1 on Kildaire Farm Road (SR 1300); parking lot on north side of road after crossing Swift Creek.*

Ownership: Town of Cary (919-469-4061) and NCDPR (919-733-4181). Triangle Land Conservancy owns nearby Swift Creek Bluffs Preserve (919-833-3662).

Size: Approximately 150 acres   **Closest Town:** Cary   **P** 🚶

Corn snakes are valuable predators, helping to control populations of rodents and other animals. PARIS TRAIL

49 | Umstead State Park

Description: Forested "island" in urban area provides habitats for many wildlife species representative of eastern piedmont region. Habitats include successional pine and mixed hardwood forests, old-growth beech slopes, and small streams and lakes. Good varieties of birdlife along with resident amphibians, reptiles, beaver and other small mammals, and white-tailed deer. Diverse spring wildflowers. Adjacent to North Carolina State University Schenck research forest, where a mixture of forests, meadows, pastures, open lake and beaver marsh create excellent habitats for great diversity of birds.

Viewing Information: Approximately twenty-three miles of foot and bridle trails in park; connecting trail system through Schenck university forest; nature study interpretive programs.

Directions: Main entrances are six miles northwest of Raleigh from U.S. 70; five miles west of Raleigh from I-40 at Cary-Harrison Ave. exit 287; and Schenck Forest access east of park on Reedy Creek Road.

Ownership: NCDPR (919-787-3033)

Size: 5,337 acres   **Closest Towns:** Raleigh and Cary

50 | Durant Nature Park

Description: City park dedicated to nature education. Variety of piedmont habitats include two small lakes, streams, meadows, and extensive pine and hardwood forests. Facilities and trails developed for environmental education. Rich variety of wildlife include more than 150 species of birds, dozens of reptiles, and amphibians, including several amphibian breeding ponds. Excellent opportunities to view a colony of beaver and abundant white-tailed deer. Feeding stations and gardens attract butterflies and birds.

Viewing Information: Full range of nature interpretive programs, with emphasis on youth environmental education. Five miles of trails. Small nature museum and wildlife rehabilitation center. Training lodge and conference facilities. Lake with swimming and boating. Group camps and outing programs.

Directions: Ten miles northeast of downtown Raleigh and two miles south of Falls Lake; northwest from U.S. 1 on Durant Road (SR 2006); watch for directional signs.

Ownership: City of Raleigh Parks and Recreation (919-847-6710 or 755-6640)

Size: 237 acres   **Closest Town:** Raleigh

51 Medoc Mountain State Park

Description: Little Fishing Creek flows along bluffs and ridges in the piedmont-coastal plain transitional area. Good examples of successional pine and mixed hardwood forests in the eastern piedmont region. Streams and wet lowlands and varied forest habitats support many animals. Diversity of birds including thrushes, vireos, and woodpeckers, hawks and owls, herons and wood ducks, along with many small mammals. The rare Carolina mudpuppy, a large aquatic salamander, inhabits the creek, along with variety of freshwater mussels, amphibians, and reptiles. Interesting assortment of spring wildflowers.

Viewing Information: Best viewed by series of hiking trails or by canoe; trailheads near park office and picnic parking lots.

Directions: Fifteen miles southwest of Roanoke Rapids and twenty-three miles north of Rocky Mount; from NC 48 turn west onto SR 1002 for 1.4 miles to park office; or from NC 561 turn east at Hollister onto SR 1002 for four miles to park office.

Ownership: NCDPR (919-445-2280)

Size: 2,287 acres   **Closest Town:** Hollister

52 Falls Lake

Description: Natural areas along shoreline and in upper flood zones of Corps of Engineers reservoir support wide variety of forest habitat and interesting geologic features. Several unique botanical sites, including B.W.Wells interpretive nature area and Pennys Bend preserve. Wildlife seen here includes river otter, muskrat, wood ducks, cormorants, and many turtles. Fish abundant in lake. Beaverdam Creek subimpoundment is good viewing site for migratory waterfowl, wading birds, and raptors, including occasional osprey and bald eagle. A well-established beaver colony in upper swamp forest. Pennys Bend preserve on lower Eno River noted for uncommon wildflowers and plentiful butterflies.

Viewing Information: North of Raleigh and east of Durham; numerous access sites, marinas, public beaches and picnic areas. Hunting occurs on some wildlife management areas in fall and winter, but never on Sundays.

Directions: Most access sites reached from NC 50 or NC 98. Obtain detailed map from management agencies. Beaverdam Lake reached southeast of Creedmoor via NC 50. Pennys Bend preserve is located upstream from SR 1004 Eno River bridge, northeast of Durham; access by permission of North Carolina Botanical Garden managers.

Ownership: USCOE; land managers NCDPR (919-846-9991), NCWRC (919-733-7291); NC Botanical Garden (919-962-0522) for Pennys Bend.

Size: 11,000-acre lake with buffer lands of 5,534 acres

Closest Towns: Raleigh and Durham

53 | Eno River State Park

Description: Small scenic river meanders through woodlands and farmlands, passing an array of piedmont natural habitats including bottomland wetlands and representative forest types. View small mammals such as beaver, river otter, mink, and muskrat. Hardwood forests support wild turkey and many songbirds, owls, and hawks. Wood ducks, great blue herons, and spotted sandpipers along water's edge. High water quality supports large populations of freshwater mussels, crayfish, many fish species, and aquatic invertebrates. Many dragonflies; exceptional displays of spring wildflowers.

Viewing Information: Few's Ford is principal visitor access point to park office and interpretive exhibits. Other road crossings and canoe access sites. Foot trails along the river.

Directions: Northwest of city of Durham; four access areas reached from I-85 by either Cole Mill Road (SR 1569) or Pleasant Green Road (SR 1567) exits. Consult detailed park maps.

Ownership: NCDPR (919-383-1686)

Size: 2,124 acres   **Closest Town:** Durham

The cascading Eno River supports diverse populations of fish, mollusks, and aquatic invertebrates. With its many ancient Indian and colonial settlement sites, the river also offers a good deal of history. WALTER C. BIGGS

Description: Duke University research forest allows public access for hiking and horseback riding, fishing, and picnicking. Forest contains some of best examples of mature forest types remaining in piedmont region. Especially interesting is the New Hope Creek corridor in forest's Korstian division, with its mixture of rocky bluffs, upland and floodplain forests, and scenic stream. Wide variety of birdlife and small mammals including otter and beaver. Floodplain pools excellent habitat for many reptiles and amphibians. Efforts underway by Triangle Land Conservancy and local governments to protect New Hope Creek and bottomland forests as an urban wildlife refuge and greenway.

Viewing Information: Extensive trails maintained in Duke Forest. Reservations required for use of picnic shelters. Contact forest manager for trail maps and use regulations (Duke University School of Environment). Approximately 800 acres of university forest reserved as protected natural areas; other areas managed for forestry and research.

Directions: Total of seven units of Duke Forest located principally west of Durham and north of Chapel Hill (see also Jordan Lake). Access points to New Hope Creek section (Korstian division) from Whitfield Road (SR 1731) on south side or Mt. Sinai Road (SR 1718) on north side, with roadside parking near marked gates.

Ownership: Duke University School of Environment (919-684-2421)

Size: 7,700 acres   **Closest Towns:** Durham and Chapel Hill   P ⊼ ⋏

Red-shouldered hawks are frequently seen in wetland forests. A wide variety of raptors appear in North Carolina during their spring and fall migrations.
KEN TAYLOR

55 | Mason Farm Biological Reserve

Description: University of North Carolina's Mason Farm Biological Reserve administered as part of the N.C. Botanical Garden. Outstanding examples of piedmont forest types and successional old fields along Morgan Creek. Steep bluffs here are covered with purple laurel. Long-term research area for rich populations of birds, amphibians, and turtles. More than 200 bird species resident or regular visitors. Other wildlife includes river otter, beaver, bobcat, gray fox, also snakes, turtles, and lizards. Wildflowers in old fields attract as many as seventy species of butterflies. Adjoins Jordan Lake wildlife management areas and the Botanical Garden educational center with interpretive and display areas.

Viewing Information: Public access restricted; permits must be obtained from NC Botanical Garden administrative office. Old dirt roads serve as foot trails. Access road fords creek. Reserve excellent place to see hawks, owls, and other birds year-round. Observe restrictions on entry into research sites.

Directions: Southeast of Chapel Hill and university campus; part of NC Botanical Garden lands.

Ownership: University of North Carolina, NC Botanical Garden (919-962-0522)

Size: 367 acres   **Closest Town:** Chapel Hill

Careful management has allowed wild turkey populations to increase throughout North Carolina. Persistance and a bit of luck are needed to view these large, wary birds in forests and along the edges of fields.
DENVER A. BRYAN

Description: Bald eagles roost and feed here in one of largest concentrations in the Mid-Atlantic region: as many as sixty birds often present in summer on Corps of Engineers reservoir. Eagles roost at upper end of the lake and forage for fish throughout region. Observation deck managed cooperatively by local Audubon Society chapter and state wildlife agency. Osprey and double-crested cormorants nest on lake. Waterfowl use lake in winter. Beaver and otter have been seen from the eagle observation platform. Annual bird counts tally up to 100 species. Haw River upstream from lake (partially in a unit of Duke University Forest) popular for whitewater canoeing.

Viewing Information: Best chance to see bald eagles between May and August. Follow marked trail 0.7 mile to eagle observation deck; trail begins at gravel parking lot on NC 751. Parking lot turnoff located about five miles south of NC 54 or 6.7 miles north of U.S. 64. BALD EAGLES STRICTLY PROTECTED BY LAW AND MUST NOT BE HARASSED. Hunting permitted in some wildlife management areas during fall and winter (except on Sundays). Park office and information center near lake on U.S. 64 west of NC 751.

Directions: Principal access from U.S. 64 causeway over lake west of Raleigh and east of Pittsboro. Other bridge crossings and numerous access points for park facilities, beaches, boat ramps, forest management demonstration area, and wildlife management areas. Detailed maps available.

Ownership: USCOE; management by NCDPR (919-362-0586) and NCWRC (919-733-7291)

Size: Lake 13,900 acres, forest lands 1,925 acres

Closest Towns: Pittsboro and Chapel Hill

This viewing platform on Jordan Lake provides an ideal vantage point for seeing the lake's large population of bald eagles. As many as sixty birds have been sighted during the summer months.

KEITH LONGIOTTI

57 Caswell Game Land

Description: This upland hardwood forest is home to the state's largest population of wild turkeys. Mature oaks and hickories, along with beech slopes and alluvial hardwood forests, represent the climax forests that once prevailed in the region. The habitats are ideal for a variety of resident woodland birds and small mammals, along with other animals typical of piedmont forests and stream habitats.

Viewing Information: Best times to visit the state game lands for wildlife observation are on non-hunting days. HUNTING OCCURS DURING FALL, WINTER, AND APRIL-MAY ON MONDAYS, WEDNESDAYS, SATURDAYS, AND HOLIDAYS. Adjacent Boy Scout Camp Cherokee is open for public use and features a system of foot trails through hardwood forests.

Directions: Site approximately twenty-five miles north of Burlington. Principal tracts of state game lands located south and east of Yanceyville; depot office on west side of NC 62 approximately two miles south of Yanceyville; Boy Scout camp to west on SR 1120 and 1121.

Ownership: NCWRC (919-694-9272 or 733-7291)

Size: all units total over 16,500 acres   **Closest Town:** Yanceyville

58 Uwharrie National Forest Sites

Description: An array of protected forest habitats on the ancient Uwharrie Mountains. Birkhead Wilderness Area in northern sector of the national forest is composed of upland forest types. Wildlife management areas and designated natural areas are scattered through the forest, particularly on the Uwharrie River and along Badin Lake. Westernmost stands of longleaf pine in the state. The forest supports wildlife representative of the central piedmont. View a wide variety of resident and migratory birds, small mammals, white-tailed deer, reptiles, and amphibians, especially in floodplains and upland seasonal ponds.

Viewing Information: Consult national forest for detailed maps. Numerous hiking trails, boat ramps, and visitor facilities.

Directions: Forest reached by NC 109.

Ownership: USFS (919-576-6391)

Size: 46,000 total acres, including 1,300-acre wilderness

Closest Towns: Troy and Asheboro

P

59 Morrow Mountain State Park

Description: Mature, second-growth forests dominated by oaks and hickories, with beech slopes and successional red cedar and pine woodlands. Alluvial hardwood forests in lowlands along the Yadkin-Pee Dee River and tributaries. Located on ancient Uwharrie Mountains, with erosion-resistant summits known as "monadnocks." Many animals move along the floodplain forest corridors. Birds abundant in all seasons; view many songbirds, raptors, flycatchers, herons, kingfisher, and woodpeckers. Interesting variety of frogs, salamanders, turtles, and many small mammals. Wide assortment of wildflowers.

Viewing Information: Over thirty miles of hiking and bridle trails; natural history museum; self-guided nature trails; scenic views.

Directions: *Between Albemarle and Badin; from junction of NC 24- 27-73-740, follow NC 740 (Badin Road) northeast about 3.6 miles to SR 1798 (Morrow Mtn Road); turn right and proceed 3.5 miles to park boundary and further to entry gate. Located on west side of river from Uwharrie National Forest.*

Ownership: NCDPR (704-982-4402)

Size: 4,693 acres   **Closest Towns:** Albemarle and Badin

P ⛺ ⛲ ⛰ 🚶

60 Pee Dee National Wildlife Refuge

Description: A mixture of diverse upland and bottomland habitats including pine forests, fields, and the largest protected expanse of bottomland hardwood forest remaining in piedmont region. Located along the Pee Dee River and its Brown Creek tributary. Wetlands support many animals. View mammals such as raccoon, white-tailed deer, opossum, eastern cottontail, southern flying squirrel, gray squirrel, river otter, and beaver. Among diverse resident birds are owls, pileated and other woodpeckers, wood duck, and many songbirds. Westernmost colony of endangered red-cockaded woodpecker in upland pine stands. Small wintering flocks of Canada geese. Large numbers of wintering mallards and black ducks.

Viewing Information: System of refuge roads and trails, small impoundments, wildlife food plots, and observation areas. Contact refuge office for detailed map.

Directions: *Reached north from Wadesboro by U.S. 52.*

Ownership: USFWS (704-694-4224)

Size: 8,443 acres   **Closest Towns:** Ansonville and Wadesboro

P 🚤

SITE NUMBER   SITE NAME

61   **Crowders Mountain**
62   **Cowans Ford Wildlife Refuge and Latta Plantation Park**
63   **Duke Power State Park**
64   **South Mountains State Park**
65   **Piedmont Environmental Center**
66   **Hanging Rock State Park**
67   **Pilot Mountain State Park**

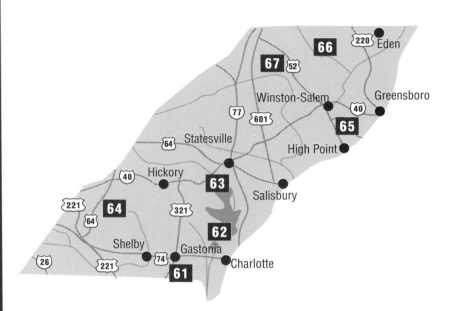

Description: With sheer vertical cliffs of quartzite, Crowders Mountain and Kings Pinnacle tower 800 feet above surrounding piedmont region. Park is forested by mature hardwoods on lower slopes and stunted chestnut oaks and pines on dry ridgetops. Rich in ferns and wildflowers. Featured wildlife includes small mammals, abundant salamanders, turtles, toads, and frogs. Over thirty species of warblers observed among the 160 birds found in the park. Black and turkey vultures roost on isolated rock outcrops and soar from peaks.

Viewing Information: Hiking trails through forest and to scenic overlooks. Nature study programs. Small boats may be rented on park lake.

Directions: *Six miles southwest of Gastonia; take exit 13 from I 85 at junction with U.S. 29/74. Turn south on SR 1125 (Sparrow Springs Road) to park.*

Ownership: NCDPR (704-867-1181)

Size: 2,364 acres   **Closest Towns:** Gastonia and Kings Mountain

Despite their vibrant colors, salamanders are reclusive creatures, dwelling under the leaf litter of forest floors or underneath rotting logs. The marbled salamander lives on land but journeys in the spring to temporal ponds to breed and lay eggs. PARIS TRAIL

With descendants dating back 350 million years, ferns are among the oldest living plants on earth. This New York fern is one of several varieties found in North Carolina.

KEN TAYLOR/N.C. WILDLIFE

62 | Cowans Ford Refuge and Latta Plantation Park

Description: Waterfowl refuge and park about six miles apart, located along eastern shore of Mountain Island Lake on the Catawba River. Cowan's Ford Refuge supports a large number of Canada geese and waterfowl in the winter. Look for nesting osprey in the summer. Deer are abundant in both areas. Latta Place, an early 19th century plantation, is the focal point of Latta Park, but the park also has an Audubon sanctuary, photo blind, and trail system for viewing wildlife. Watch for osprey in the summer and wading birds year-round. Canoe access in the park. Waterbirds such as loons, grebes, and gulls can be seen in the deep water of Lake Norman near the dam.

Viewing Information: On Cowans Ford Refuge, viewing opportunities excellent for waterfowl during winter at viewing stand found at end of road into refuge. Deer often seen in fields of the refuge and Latta Park. Wading birds and osprey often seen on the lake. Canoeing backwater areas of the lake a good way to see waterfowl, osprey, turtles, and other wildlife.

Directions: *To Cowans Ford Refuge from I-77, take NC 73 west to Beatties Ford Road (SR 2128), then south to Neck Road (SR 2074); then west to refuge viewing stand. To Latta Plantation Park follow directions to refuge but continue on Beatties Ford Road (SR 2128/2074 south) to Sample Road (SR 2125); west on Sample Road to park entrance.*

Ownership: Mecklenburg County Parks (704-875-1391); Duke Power Company

Size: 1,600 acres total   **Closest Towns:** Charlotte and Huntersville

White-tailed deer are common in fields and woodlands throughout North Carolina. Early morning and dusk are good times to view deer as they move into open areas to feed. KEN TAYLOR

63 Duke Power State Park

Description: Located on northern shore of Lake Norman, the largest manmade lake in state. Forested primarily by successional pines with pockets of hardwood forest and moist lowland forests along streams and lake coves. Lake known for large numbers of freshwater fish. Amphibians and reptiles abundant, with greatest variety of turtles, frogs, and water snakes inhabiting wetlands along shoreline and in creeks. Mammals and birdlife typical of the region. More than thirty species of small mammals found here, but rarely seen. Osprey commonly viewed fishing; red-tailed hawks over the lake. Recent hurricane downed many trees and created ideal habitat for great numbers of woodpeckers. Lake attracts wood ducks, mallards, teal, and other waterfowl. Watch for herons and egrets along shallow waters.

Viewing Information: Side roads lead to many lake access points. Two hiking trails—easy 0.8 mile Alder Trail and 2.5 or 5.4 mile Lakeshore Trail loops—facilitate wildlife viewing.

Directions: Ten miles south of Statesville; from I-77 to Troutman, exit U.S. 21 in Troutman at park sign and proceed west on Wagner Road (SR 1321) and State Park Road (SR 1330) four miles to park's main entrance.

Ownership: NCDPR (704-528-6350)

Size: 1,447 acres   **Closest Towns:** Troutman and Statesville

P 🏚 ♿ ⛽ ⛺ 🚶 🛶 🚤

64 South Mountains State Park

Description: Located in extreme western piedmont region. Cove hardwood forests rich in wildflowers and ferns. Dry ridges covered by pines and oaks with heath understory. Numerous cascades and waterfalls. Bird life is abundant, with sixty nesting species observed. Some more typical of mountains such as ruffed grouse, black-throated green warblers, and rose-breasted grosbeaks. Common ravens nest on rock ledges. White-tailed deer plentiful, along with many smaller mammals. Variety of salamanders, frogs, toads, and reptiles.

Viewing Information: Network of new hiking trails and old CCC and logging roads serve as hiking and bridle trails. Wildlife abundant but not easily seen.

Directions: Eighteen miles south of Morganton; leave I-40 at exit 105 and take NC 18 south about ten miles. Turn right on SR 1913 for 3.5 miles, then left on SR 1924 for two miles. Turn right on SR 1901 for about 1.5 miles, then right onto SR 1904 for 3.6 miles to park entrance.

Ownership: NCDPR (704-433-4772)

Size: 7,226 acres   **Closest Town:** Morganton

P 🏚 ⛽ ⛺ 🚶

65 | Piedmont Environmental Center

Description: Located on northern shore of High Point Lake. A patchwork of upland pine and hardwood forests, old fields, floodplain forest on Deep River, and cattail marsh on margins of the lake. Good natural exhibit of all stages of piedmont vegetational succession. Open pastures mowed to maintain wildlife habitats. Representation of wildlife common to the piedmont including songbirds, owls, woodpeckers, and bobwhite quail. Also white-tailed deer, river otter, grey fox, and other small mammals, and as many as twenty species of reptiles and amphibians.

Viewing Information: Center offers many nature education classes and field studies. Traversed by 6.5 miles of trails with observation stops, a boardwalk across the cattail marsh, and a floating bridge over a bay of the lake.

Directions: Southwest of Greensboro; south from I-40 at Wendover, go two miles southwest on Wendover Ave. (SR 1541), turn left on Penny Rd. (SR 1536) to signed entry near north shore of High Point Lake.

Ownership: City of High Point and Environmental Center (919-454- 4214)

Size: 376 acres   **Closest Town:** High Point and Jamestown   P 🏛 ⛱ 🚶

State parks like Hanging Rock offer fine views, hiking trails, and numerous wildlife viewing opportunities. Most parks also feature nature interpretive programs and wildlife checklists. KEN TAYLOR/N.C. WILDLIFE

Description: Isolated group of low mountains with exceptional diversity of forest communities. Impressive quartzite-capped ridges and cliffs. Mixture of piedmont and montane flora. Cascading streams and waterfalls in narrow ravines. Extension of park reaches nearby Dan River. Wildlife typical of piedmont and mountain foothills. Birds abundant year-round, with greatest numbers seen during spring and fall migrations. Variety of frogs and toads, lizards, snakes, and salamanders including the state's only population of Wehrle's salamander. Commonly seen mammals include white-tailed deer, foxes, raccoons, and bats.

Viewing Information: More than eighteen miles of hiking trails to many scenic areas and habitat types. Trails lead to waterfalls, scenic overlooks, and a remote cave.

Directions: *Four miles west of Danbury; entrance from SR 1001 (Moore's Spring Road) that connects between NC 89 east of park and NC 66 west of park.*

Ownership: NCDPR (919-593-8480)

Size: 6,194 acres   **Closest Town:** Danbury   P 🏠 ♿ ⛽ ⛺ 🚶 🛶

67 | **Pilot Mountain State Park**

Description: Spectacular rock summit of Big Pinnacle towers above surrounding countryside. Cliffs favored nesting areas for ravens and turkey vultures. Occasional visits by peregrine falcon. Good vista for viewing fall migrations of raptors. Other resident fauna typical of western piedmont and mountain foothills. Attached park unit on Yadkin River is covered by floodplain forest providing an important corridor and with ponds serving as breeding habitat for many frogs and salamanders. Provides boating access to popular recreational and scenic river.

Viewing Information: Travelers on U.S. 52 see rock pinnacle from many miles away. Variety of park foot trails on Little and Big Pinnacles, and Yadkin River section. Two-mile section of river flows by park, part of a popular 165-mile canoe trail. Sauratown Trail connects Pilot Mountain to Hanging Rock park.

Directions: *Fourteen miles south of Mount Airy and twenty-four miles north of Winston Salem; Pilot Mountain park section midway between towns of Pinnacle and Pilot Mountain on west side of U.S. 52; exit onto SR 2053 to main park entry. Yadkin River section 8.2 miles from U.S. 52 on SR 2065-2072.*

Ownership: NCDPR (919-325-2355)

Size: 3,703 acres   **Closest Towns:** Pinnacle and Pilot Mountain

P 🏠 ♿ ⛽ ⛺ 🚶 🛶

Southern Appalachian Mountains

The mountain region is defined by a dramatic "front" or escarpment rising as much as 2,000 feet above the adjacent Piedmont lowlands. The Blue Ridge mountains extend 250 miles along the eastern front of this region through North Carolina. The Appalachian mountains reach their highest elevations here, with forty-three peaks surpassing 6,000 feet in elevation. Mount Mitchell, with a 6,684-foot summit, is the tallest peak in eastern America. Impressive today, these mountains are merely eroded foundations of peaks that once matched the heigths of the mountain ranges in western North America.

The mountains are covered by lush forests with an extraordinary diversity of wildlife. The cool conditions of the high peaks harbor animals and plants more commonly seen in northern latitudes, such as spruce-fir boreal forests and rich mixtures of northern hardwood trees. The Southern Appalachians are known for large numbers of species native only to this region. Unusual treeless areas, known as mountaintop "balds," are covered by heath shrubs like rhododendrons and laurels, or by grasses and shrubs. The natural communities of the mountains also include hemlock forests, uncommon bogs and fens, and "cove forests" which support a variety of wildlife unequaled in eastern North America.

Looking northwest from the summit of Mount Mitchell KEN TAYLOR

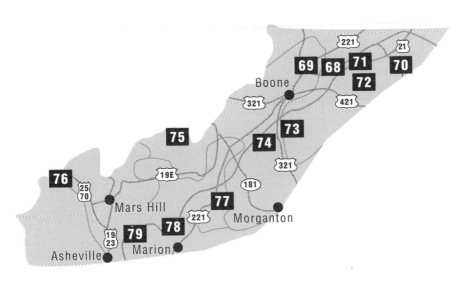

68 New River State Park

Description: Geologically the oldest river in North America. Many fish species not found elsewhere in the state. View muskrat, beaver, mink, raccoon, and white-tailed deer near river. Salamanders, turtles, frogs, and water snakes common. Good population of hellbender salamanders found in the river. Variety of woodland birds and ducks. Watch for osprey and red-tailed hawks. Wild turkey and grouse common on uplands near the river.

Viewing Information: Several river access points in park. Canoe rentals nearby. 26.5 miles designated state Natural and Scenic River.

Directions: East and north of Jefferson; Wagoner Road park access reached eight miles southeast of Jefferson off NC 88 via SR 1590; U.S. 221 park access further upstream; other access points under development.

Ownership: NCDPR (919-982-2587)
Size: 1,089 acres   **Closest Town:** Jefferson

69 Mount Jefferson State Park

Description: Upper slopes of 4,683-foot mountain summit support mature northern hardwood forest with stands of uncommon bigtooth aspen. Fine examples of oak-hickory forest on lower slopes. Numerous rare plants. Animals typical of region, including common small mammals and more secretive mice and shrews. View a variety of songbirds here, including warblers, thrushes, flycatchers, wrens, grosbeaks, and tanagers. Also view variety of hawks during fall migration.

Viewing Information: Self-guided nature trail to summit from parking area and picnic ground; panoramic views from overlooks.

Directions: Entrance from U.S. 221 midway between Jefferson and West Jefferson; exit east on SR 1152 for 1.5 mi. to park gate and two miles to summit parking lot. Blue Ridge Parkway about fifteen miles east of Mount Jefferson by way of NC 16 or NC 163.

Ownership: NCDPR (919-246-9653) Size: **489 acres Closest Town**: Jefferson

Smart rabbits stay close to brier patches and other protective cover, or else they may become a meal for a fox, hawk, or other predators. WILLIAM S. LEA

Description: Massive granite dome on edge of Blue Ridge Escarpment. Rounded cliffs rise 600 feet above base. Pockets of soil support pioneer plants. Forest habitats suited to dry conditions here, with cove hardwood forests on lower slopes. Abundant birdlife and mammals. Black bear and bobcat rarely seen. More easily observed animals include wild turkey, white-tailed deer, gray and red foxes, gray squirrels, raccoons, and opossums. Similar habitats may be found in adjacent Thurmond Chatham state game land.

Viewing Information: Park is divided by John Frank Parkway (SR 1784); network of park hiking trails with most popular on south side of Stone Mtn.; additional park trails follow Widows and Garden Creeks. State gamelands contain foot and jeep trails open only through hunting season. Best times to visit state game lands are on non-hunting days. HUNTING OCCURS DURING FALL, WINTER, AND APRIL-MAY ON MONDAYS THROUGH SATURDAYS AND HOLIDAYS.

Directions: East of Blue Ridge Parkway. From U.S. 21 turn west on SR 1002 and go about four miles to Traphill, turn north on parkway (SR 1784) and continue 2.5 mi. to park entrance. Access to game lands from the Parkway at Air Bellows Gap (milepost 237.5) or from south via NC 18 and SR 1728-1730.

Ownership: NCDPR (919-957-8185), NCWRC (919-733-7291)

Size: Park 13,434 acres, game land 7,052 acres

Closest Towns: Midway between Sparta and Elkin

P🏠🏕⛰🚶

Common in all woodlands, the gray squirrel is often seen hard at work, collecting acorns and other nuts which it stores in preparation for winter. Watch for the more secretive fox squirrel and the nocturnal flying squirrel too. WILLIAM S. LEA

71 | Blue Ridge Parkway

Description: From Shenandoah National Park in Virginia to Great Smoky Mountains National Park in North Carolina, the Blue Ridge Parkway is a 470-mile scenic motorway down the crest of the Blue Ridge Mountains. It passes through an array of habitat types and elevations ranging from 2,000 to over 6,000 feet. Highest elevations feature natural communities similar to those found in New England. During the day, look for chipmunks, groundhogs, squirrels, and occasional white-tailed deer. Black bear present but seldom seen. At night watch for striped and spotted skunks, bobcats, foxes, opossums, and raccoons along roadsides. Parkway follows major migration route for birds and monarch butterflies. Warblers plentiful in spring and summer along with many other resident birds. Several breeding colonies of the rare cerulean warbler.

Viewing Information: Many roadside pulloffs, overlooks, trails, self-guided nature walks, visitor services, nature programs, museums and roadside exhibits. Most popular for displays of flowers and blooms of laurel, azalea, and rhododendron in late spring and early summer, or for the blaze of leaf colors in autumn. PARKWAY MAY BE CLOSED FOR EXTENDED PERIODS IN THE WINTER DUE TO SNOW AND ICE. NO WILDLIFE VIEWING SIGNS ARE POSTED ALONG THE PARKWAY.

Directions: From Virginia down Blue Ridge Mountain chain, crosses I-40 outside Asheville, and ends in Great Smoky Mountains National Park.

Ownership: NPS (704-259-0779)

Size: 255 miles in North Carolina

Some animals have suffered as a result of human encroachment, but raccoons have prospered. These adaptable mammals are seen from cypress swamps and mountains to suburban yards.
KEN TAYLOR

72 Blue Ridge Parkway: Doughton Park

Description: One of the larger tracts along Parkway contains forest habitats representative of the northern Blue Ridge mountains. Good place to see white-tailed deer. Several overlooks good places to view many hawks, songbirds, and monarch butterflies during fall migrations. Ravens often observed soaring over rocky areas, such as Alligator Back. Bobcats present but rarely seen, though their signs easily located. Wildcat Rocks named for bobcat dens there. Black bear is a rare but seldom seen resident. Wild turkey common. Abundant populations of snakes and lizards. A pond near the parkway harbors beaver and wood duck. The trail to Fodderstack Mountain passes rare bigtooth aspen and Carolina hemlock.

Viewing Information: Network of thirty miles of trails; see trail system signboard at Alligator Back Overlook, milepost 242.2. Campground and lodge. Wildlife viewing excellent spring through fall. Use caution driving at night—deer often cross roads.

Directions: *Two miles east of BRP junction with NC 18; between BRP milepost 238.5-244.7; west of Stone Mountain State Park.*

Ownership: NPS (919-372-8867)

Size: 6,000 acres   **Closest Town:** Laurel Springs

73 Blue Ridge Parkway: Moses Cone and Julian Price Parks

Description: These former estates contain hardwood, hemlock, birch forests, pastures, and impounded lakes. Set of unique mountain bogs with wetland shrubs and sedges. These diverse habitats support a variety of wildlife, including a great diversity of birds. Hemlock and hardwood forest around Trout Lake notable for breeding songbirds such as Blackburnian and Canada warblers, and rose-breasted grosbeaks. Sapsuckers breed in the area. The hardwood forest near the Cone Manor contains many wildflowers.

Viewing Information: Thirty-five miles of trails loop from manor house, campgrounds, lakes, and picnic areas. Several popular fishing lakes.

Directions: *West of BRP junction with U.S. 221 outside Blowing Rock and south of Boone; adjoining tracts extend from mileposts 292.7-300.*

Ownership: NPS (704-295-7591)

Size: 7,860 acres   **Closest Town:** Blowing Rock

74 | Grandfather Mountain

Description: Famous for spectacular rocky profiles. Rich hardwood forests on slopes; heath balds and spruce-fir forests on summits. Great biological diversity here, including many rare plants and animals. Excellent location to observe migratory hawks and warblers. View peregrine falcons most of the year, also ravens soaring. Site features habitat for northern animal species such as saw-whet owl, black-capped chickadee, winter wren, golden-crowncd kinglet, veery, brown creeper, northern flying squirrel, and New England cottontail. Eastern wood rats found in crevices of rock outcrops. One of region's most impressive sites for salamanders, with sixteen species found here.

Viewing Information: Ten trails with convenient access. Auto route from U.S. 221 to mountain top at "Mile High Swinging Bridge" area. Fees charged for admission and for hiking permits. Permits available at main gate (east of Linville on U.S. 221) and other area stores. Tanawha trail runs about thirteen miles along Blue Ridge Parkway on eastern flank of Grandfather Mountain. This is last completed section of Parkway and includes famous Linn Cove Viaduct. HIKERS MUST STAY ON THE TRAILS. A new nature museum near summit is next to a wildlife viewing area featuring bear, deer, eagles, cougar, and other native species.

Directions: Bounded by BR Parkway on east, U.S. 221 on south, and NC 105 on west. From Parkway take Linville exit for U.S. 221 at MP 305, about one mile south of BRP Viaduct visitors center. Short distance to entrance for drive to Grandfather Mountain summit from U.S. 221.

Additional Viewing Opportunities: Explore trails and wildlife viewing sites on nearby national forest lands, including Wilson Creek area and proposed Harpers Creek and Lost Cove wildernesses.

Ownership: Grandfather Mountain, Inc. (800-468-7325) and NPS (704-765-2761)

Size: Approximately 2,000 acres   **Closest Town:** Linville   P🏠🅿$⛽🚹

The Southern Appalachian mountains are characterized by clear-running streams, such as this waterfall on Grandfather Mountain. Streams offer prime wildlife viewing for many birds, amphibians, and mammals.
KEN TAYLOR

75 Roan Mountain

Description: Most extensive heath and grassy balds on Roan Mountain ridgecrest. Beautiful vistas and flowers along ten-mile segment of Appalachian Trail, often called most scenic segment of the trail. Northern flying squirrel, New England cottontail, and saw-whet owl are near southern extent of ranges. Also present are least weasel, spotted skunk, black bear, bobcat, mice, and salamanders. Ravens, hawks, and occasional golden eagles seen over balds and cliffs.

Viewing Information: Auto access to massive "garden" of purple rhododendron and flame azalea, with short trails to spruce-fir forest and clifftops on Roan High Knob. Best means of viewing grass and heath balds by walking segments of Appalachian Trail east from Carvers Gap.

Directions: Sixteen miles north of Bakersville on Tennessee state line; reached via NC 261 or TN 143 (upslope from TN Roan Mountain State Park). At Carvers Gap follow two-mile spur road (SR 1348) to Roan summit and parking for trailhead.

Additional Viewing Opportunities: Nolichucky River gorge and Big Bald mountain on nearby national forest lands.

Ownership: USFS (704-682-6146), TNC (919-967-7007), and Southern Appalachian Highlands Conservancy (615-434-2555)
Size: 10,000 acres   **Closest Towns:** Bakersville in NC, Roan Mountain in TN

76 French Broad River Natural Areas

Description: Numerous natural areas and hiking trails near the French Broad River, largest river in western NC. Scenic natural areas such as Big Laurel Creek and Spring Creek gorge feature rare wildlife. Full range of Southern Appalachian wildlife here. Wild turkey often seen. Rich Mountain bear sanctuary north of river.

Viewing Information: Contact district ranger for trail, access, and camping information. River and natural areas accommodate auto tours, bicycling, canoeing, rafting, and hiking. Scenic overlooks of Spring Creek gorge along NC 209. Big Laurel gorge, east of Hot Springs, has hiking access from U.S. 70. EXTREMELY RUGGED TERRAIN WITH FRAGILE NATURAL AREAS. STAY ON ESTABLISHED TRAILS, WATERWAYS, AND ROADS.

Directions: Sites of interest surround the town of Hot Springs on the French Broad River; access from U.S. 70/25 from Asheville and Newport, TN; and from NC 209 from Waynesville.

Ownership: USFS (704-622-3202)   **Size:** Special-interest areas within a 14,000-acre district. Big Laurel natural area is more than 300 acres.
Closest Town: Hot Springs

77 Linville Gorge and Falls

Description: In this national wilderness area, the Linville River plunges ninety feet as it enters the deepest gorge in eastern America. Habitat includes old-growth hemlock and white pine, and mixed cove and northern hardwood forests on lower slopes. Stands of oaks and pines on gorge's dry rim. Chimneys area near Table Rock parking lot is good place to view peregrine falcons during most of the year. Numerous turkey vultures and some black vultures present. Ravens commonly seen soaring. Eastern wood rats found among rock outcrops. Red foxes often seen. The hemlock stands at falls feature breeding birds usually associated with spruce-fir forests, such as red-breasted nuthatch. Red crossbills infrequently seen. Large numbers of snakes and lizards, also many amphibians. Fine vantage points to observe fall migrating birds and monarch butterflies.

Viewing Information: Four short nature trails in area of falls from NPS parking lots. Wilderness trails descend into lower gorge. Scenic vistas on eastern and western rims of gorge accessible by roads. Permits from USFS required for wilderness camping.

Directions: Access to waterfalls from BR Parkway milepost 316.5 at end of 1.2 mile spur road; or from NC 181 on SR 1230 to eastern rim of gorge; or from NC 181 on Kistler road (SR 1238) to dramatic vista at Wiseman's View on western rim of gorge.

Additional Viewing Opportunities: Linville Caverns offers fee admission to largest limestone cave in state, with interesting cave fauna. South on U.S. 221.

Ownership: USFS (704-652-2144) and NPS (704-765-2761)

Size: 11,400 acres   **Closest Town:** Linville Falls

North Carolina's most commonly seen carnivore, the red fox is found throughout the state. Living near forests, the red fox prefers to hunt in open fields, where it pursues mice, birds, and rabbits. WILLIAM S. LEA

78 | Mount Mitchell and Black Mountains

Description: Highest mountain in eastern America at 6,684 feet. Spruce-fir trees here are dying; acid rain, disease, and insect infestation are blamed. Numerous boreal plants and animals uncommon to region survive on high-elevation islands of Canadian life zones as remnants of Ice Age. Habitat for northern flying squirrel and New England cottontail, and other more typical Southern Appalachian wildlife like deer, black bear, striped and spotted skunks, woodchuck, bobcat, and gray fox. Also view chipmunks, shrews, mice, voles, and salamanders. Breeding birds typical of northern conifer forests: saw-whet owl, red-breasted nuthatches, brown creepers, winter wrens, and golden-crowned kinglets. Excellent viewing of migratory hawks and monarch butterflies.

Viewing Information: State park on Mount Mitchell. Observation tower on summit. Interpretive center exhibits and summer programs. Rugged hiking trail from Mount Mitchell eight miles to Celo Knob. Shorter loop trails within state park. Strenuous hiking trails from summit to Black Mountain Recreation Area in Toe River valley; trail is six miles downslope.

Directions: *State park access via NC 128 spur to Mount Mitchell summit from Blue Ridge Parkway, turn at milepost 355.4, thirty-three miles north on Parkway from Asheville.*

Additional Viewing Opportunites: Nearby national forest sites offering wildlife resources include Carolina Hemlocks and South Toe River recreation area. Crabtree Meadows park and waterfall on BR Parkway at milepost 339.

Ownership: NCDPR (704-675-4611), USFS (704-682-6146), and NPS (704-259-0701)

Size: 1,677 acres in park, 3,240 acres in natural area

Closest Town: Celo

This sickly spruce-fur forest atop Mount Mitchell is a sign of environmental trouble. Already weakened by air pollution, the trees here have been stricken by insect infestation.
KEN TAYLOR/N.C. WILDLIFE

79 | Craggy Mountains and Craggy Gardens

Description: Cross-section of habitats in Blue Ridge mountains feature old-growth cove and northern hardwood forests, hemlock stands, dwarfed beech and birch forests, spruce-fir forest, and heath balds on upper elevations. Rhododendron and other heath shrubs cover flanks of the Pinnacle and Craggy Dome. Purple rhododendrons flower in mid-June. Many rare plants. Wildlife on the upper summits and lower mountain slopes and coves represent the full diversity of Southern Appalachian species. Among the more notable animals are the uncommon alder flycatcher and several rare species of shrews. Good viewing for hawks.

Viewing Information: Trails to 700-acre natural rhododendron gardens and pinnacle from Craggy Gardens overlook and picnic area. Watershed south of parkway closed to public access. FRAGILE PLANT LIFE; STAY ON TRAILS. Exhibits at BRP Craggy Gardens visitor center. PARKWAY CLOSED DURING PERIODS OF WINTER SNOW AND ICE.

Directions: South of Mount Mitchell and along BR Parkway from milepost 363.4-369.6; visitor center at mile post 364.5; spur road to picnic area at mile post 367.6.

Ownership: USFS (704-682-6146), NPS (704-765-2761), and Asheville-Buncombe Water Authority

Size: approx. 2,500 acres   **Closest Town:** Asheville   P 🏕 🪧 🚶

Ablaze with rhododendron blooms, Craggy Dome offers spectacular wildflower displays in May and June. WILLIAM S. LEA

SITE   SITE
NUMBER   NAME

80   **Hickory Nut Gorge—Chimney Rock Park**
81   **Green River Game Land**
82   **Mount Pisgah**
83   **Pink Beds**
84   **Blue Ridge Parkway: Graveyard Fields**
85   **Whitewater Falls and Gorge**
86   **Whiteside Mountain**
87   **Chattooga River Gorge—Ellicott Rock Wilderness**
88   **Standing Indian Mountain—Nantahala River Wetlands**
89   **Joyce Kilmer Memorial Forest—Slickrock Wilderness**
90   **Great Smoky Mountains National Park**

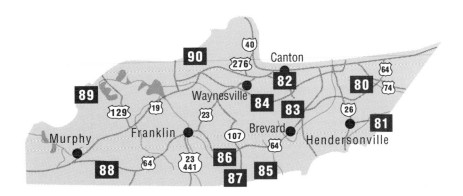

80 Hickory Nut Gorge—Chimney Rock Park

Description: Steep slopes and rock cliffs rising 1,400 feet above Broad River. Scenic Hickory Nut Falls located in privately-owned Chimney Rock Park. High bird diversity; view many warblers, including cerulean and Swainson's warblers. Excellent year-round viewing for peregrine falcons. Black vultures and ravens also seen. Elevated trails offer prime viewing of migratory songbirds at treetop level. Bottomless Pools nearby is a set of large "potholes" on Pool Creek. Bat Cave, open only for Nature Conservancy tours, is largest fissure cave in North America. Uncommon salamanders and bats found in cave and crevices.

Viewing Information: Chimney Rock Park open to public for admission fee, with nature trails to Hickory Nut Falls and scenic overlooks. Bat Cave tours by reservation only; sign up at Apple House in Bat Cave June-August.

Directions: Access to Chimney Rock Park on U.S. 64-74 in town of Chimney Rock.

Ownership: Chimney Rock Park (800-277-9611), TNC (919-967-7007), and PVT

Size: Approximately 2,000 acres   **Closest Towns:** Chimney Rock and Bat Cave

P 🏛🚻 $ ♿ ⛱ 🚶

81 Green River Game Land

Description: River flows through rugged gorge on southern Blue Ridge escarpment. Wildlife often seen include white-tailed deer, wild turkey, raccoon, gray and red fox, opossum, gray and red squirrels, and woodchuck. Common amphibians include the northern dusky and blackbelly salamanders, green frogs, gray treefrogs, and spring peepers. Commonly seen reptiles are box turtles, racers and ringneck snakes, eastern garter and black rat snakes. Cerulean warblers may be heard below the falls. Scarlet tanagers, black-throated green warblers, and worm-eating warblers among the many forest songbirds.

Viewing Information: Access to state game land by SR 1151. Also foot trail to Bradley Falls from SR 1142. Best times to visit state game lands are on non-hunting days. HUNTING OCCURS FALL, WINTER, AND APRIL-MAY ON MONDAYS THROUGH SATURDAYS AND HOLIDAYS.

Directions: Southeast from Hendersonville on I-26; take exit 28 at Saluda and then SR 1151 north; road parallels river until reaching one of several parking areas along the river.

Ownership: NCWRC (919-733-7291) and PVT

Size: Approximately 6,000 acres owned by WRC; 28,500-acre game land leased from private owners

Closest Town: Saluda

P 🚶 🛶

Description: Located along Blue Ridge Parkway, with foot trail to 5,721-foot summit. Trail passes through mature northern red oak forests, stunted beech forest, and mountain laurel heath bald. View wildlife typical of region: red squirrel, white-tailed deer, occasional black bear, and bobcat. The area is part of the Pisgah bear sanctuary. Variety of birds such as raven, ruffed grouse, winter wren, golden-crowned kinglet, rose-breasted grosbeak, towhee, junco, chickadee, and nuthatch. Hawks also seen. Site is part of George Vanderbilt's original 125,000-acre Biltmore Estate, purchased for first national forest in South. Unique mountain bog with unusual flora near campground on west side of Parkway from Pisgah Inn.

Viewing Information: Parking lot for trail access at BRP milepost 407.9. Trails also lead along margin of Pisgah bog from campground at BRP milepost 408.6. Fall brings migrating hawks and monarch butterflies.

Directions: Located near the Blue Ridge Parkway's Mount Pisgah Inn and campground. Parking for trailhead to Mount Pisgah from picnic parking lot at milepost 407.6.

Additional Viewing Opportunities: Other wildlife viewing areas nearby in national forest are the Lake Powhatan recreation area and NC Arboretum in the Bent Creek Experimental Forest southwest of Asheville; exit milepost 393.6 on NC 191.

Ownership: NPS (704-456-9530) and USFS (704-877-3350)

Size: 325 acres   **Closest Town:** Cruso   P ⦿ ⊨ ⟨ ⊼ ▲ ⟨

Just eight inches tall, the saw-whet owl is North Carolina's smallest owl, and one of the rarest. Saw-whet owls live in spruce-fur forest above 5,000 feet and are threatened by logging, pollution, and insect infestations.

TERRY SHANKLE/N.C. WILDLIFE

83 Pink Beds

Description: Part of the Cradle of Forestry Interpretive Area. Site features most extensive system of upland valley bogs in Southern Appalachians. Natural area laced with streams and small bogs dominated by shrubs and scattered trees. Wetlands harbor many rare plants such as swamp pink. Black bear sanctuary. Deer also abundant. Excellent for bird watching and viewing amphibians.

Viewing Information: Interpretive trails and numerous points of interest in vicinity; trails from Cradle of Forestry interpretive center and picnic area; obtain detailed maps at Cradle of Forestry Visitors Center or district ranger's office.

Directions: Northwest about fifteen miles from Brevard and south of Blue Ridge Parkway on U.S. 276; exit milepost 411.9 onto Wagon Road Gap; entrances marked from highway.

Additional Viewing Opportunities: Forest Heritage Scenic Byway along Davidson River and U.S. 276 leads to other points of interest. Near NCWRC fish hatchery. Wildlife viewing along complex of nearby hiking trails, including thirty-mile Art Loeb Trail and Looking Glass Rock Trail.

Ownership: USFS (704-877-3350)

Size: Approximately 1,000 acres   **Closest Town:** Brevard

84 Blue Ridge Parkway: Graveyard Fields

Description: Graveyard fields and ridge are scene of recovering forest devastated by timbering and Big Fire of 1925. Site is now covered by heath and blueberries, visited by black bear and many birds. Shrubs and saplings provide habitat for southernmost population of alder flycatchers. Parking area is good spot to watch fall flights of raptors. Open brushy habitats attract harriers and other raptors during fall migration. Good place to see golden eagles during winter. Excellent viewing of white-tailed deer.

Viewing Information: Easy walks from Parkway pulloffs, such as 3.2 mile Graveyard Fields loop trail from parking lot at milepost 418.8 or from Black Balsam parking area end of FS road 816 1.2 miles from BRP mp 420.2 to grassy balds above Ivestor Gap for dramatic vistas. Contact district forest ranger (704-877-3350) for detailed maps and hiking permits for adjacent Shining Rock Wilderness Area.

Directions: On western side of Blue Ridge Parkway, with overlooks for Yellowstone Falls at milepost 418.3, Graveyard Fields at milepost 418.8. At milepost 421.7, turn for spur road to wilderness trailheads.

Ownership: NPS (704-465-9530)

Size: Approximately 2,000 acres adjacent to larger 13,400-acre wilderness area

Closest Town: Rosman

Description: River gorge cuts through Blue Ridge escarpment with set of spectacular waterfalls. Upper Falls on North Carolina side drops 411 feet, and Lower Falls in South Carolina drops 400 feet. Forest of mixed old-growth hardwoods, white pine and hemlock. Look for a variety of songbirds including Swainson's warblers. Area noted for diversity of wildflowers and mosses. Enjoy spring and summer wildflowers along trails and at picnic area. Amphibians abundant in springs and streams.

Viewing Information: Overlooks for Upper Falls reached by short walkway from parking/picnicking area off NC 281. Best opportunities for viewing songbirds and other wildlife in old-growth forests along the Foothills Trail, a rugged seventy-five-mile hiking trail that crosses east-west over a series of river gorges to Oconee and Table Rock state parks in South Carolina.

Directions: *East of Cashiers turn south from U.S. 64 in Sapphire on NC 281, then 8.6 miles to Whitewater Falls entrance; or south from Cashiers via NC 107 and east on SC 413, then north on SC 130 which becomes NC 281 at the South Carolina state line. Directional signs from NC 281.*

Ownership: USFS (704-526-3765)

Size: 315 acres   **Closest Town:** Sapphire   P ⌂ ⅌ ⼐

Of all the many beautiful waterfalls in the state, Whitewater Falls near Cashiers is most spectacular. This set of double falls cascades more than 400 feet and is thought to be the highest falls in the Blue Ridge Mountains. KEVIN ADAMS

86 | Whiteside Mountain

Description: Peregrine falcons and ravens nest on mountain's sheer rock walls rising 2,100 feet above valleys. Forest types include Canadian and Carolina hemlock, beech, dwarf northern red oak, and dry pine-oak habitats. Located on headwaters of Chattooga river, a designated wild and scenic river. Many species of forest-dwelling songbirds viewed here. Also raptors including red-tailed and broad-wing hawks, turkey vulture, and occasional golden eagle. Wet rock outcrops along the trail inhabited by salamanders such as the mountain dusky, Jordan's, and other species.

Viewing Information: Two miles of walking trails and observation points circle the summit from parking area.

Directions: West of Cashiers and east 5.4 miles from Highlands; access from U.S. 64 at county line, turn south on Wildcat Ridge Rd. (SR 1600) and then one mile to trailhead parking lot.

Additional Viewing Opportunities: Panthertown Valley and Bonas Defeat Gorge on Tuckasegee River northeast of Cashiers are spectacular geologic landforms and natural areas in the same national forest district.

Ownership: USFS (704-526-3765)   **Size:** Approximately 2,000 acres

Closest Towns: Cashiers and Highlands   **P** 人

87 | Chattooga River Gorge—Ellicott Rock Wilderness

Description: River cuts down Blue Ridge escarpment in descent to piedmont region of South Carolina and Georgia. Gorge slopes covered by hardwood forests. Ellicott Rock marks tri-state border along the course of the national wild and scenic river. Wildlife is typical of the Southern Appalachian mountains. Watch for a wide variety of songbirds.

Viewing Information: Two miles of riverside trails from Bull Pen Road (FS 1178) bridge crossing; or several longer hiking trails (seven miles round-trip) into wilderness south from Bull Pen Road parking pullovers.

Directions: Southeast from town of Highlands on Horse Cove Rd. Pass Highlands Biological Station nature center and botanical gardens on SR 1603 on outskirts of town. Turn right on Bull Pen Road (SR 1178) which crosses river above the wilderness area and proceeds eastward to junction with NC 107 at Highlands Biological Station's Dulany Bog preserve.

Ownership: USFS (704-526-3765)

Size: approx. 4,000 acres   **Closest Town:** Highlands

88 Standing Indian Mountain— Nantahala River Wetlands

Description: High mountain ridges and summits support mature forest habitats. From wetlands near Nantahala River to highest ridges and summits, varied habitats support full range of Southern Appalachian wildlife including bear, deer, wild boar, turkey, grouse, hawks, and owls. Unique bogs, swamps, marshes, and seepages along the upper course of Nantahala River feature large number of salamanders, frogs, and turtles, as well as rare plants.

Viewing Information: Hiking trails from Standing Indian campground, or forest road to upper elevation trailhead. Area crossed by the Appalachian Trail and network of side trails. Whiteoak Bottoms Bog downstream from Standing Indian campground. No established trails into bogs. Check maps at campground or trailhead information shelters.

Directions: *West from Franklin on U.S. 64, turn south on USFS road 71-1 nearly to the summit or take old hwy 64 and USFS road 67-1 to Standing Indian Campground.*

Additional Viewing Opportunities: Wayah Bald to the north on SR 1310, and Buck Creek, Fires Creek, Cherokee Lake, Lake Chatuge, and Hiawassee Lake west of Standing Indian on U.S. 64.

Ownership: USFS (704-524-4410)

Size: 13,000 acres   **Closest Town:** Rainbow Springs   P 🏠 🛖 ⛰ 🚶

89 Joyce Kilmer Memorial Forest—Slickrock Wilderness

Description: Adjacent to a wilderness area, this memorial forest contains one of best examples of a Southern Appalachian old-growth climax forest dominated by massive cove hardwoods and Canadian hemlock, and carpeted by mosses and liverworts. Higher on slopes the forest varies from mixed northern hardwoods to dry ridgetop associations of oaks and pine with heath understory. View wildlife representative of Southern Appalachian region: bear, fox, deer, wild boar, grouse, wild turkey, owls, hawks, ravens, and many songbirds. Good habitat for salamanders.

Viewing Information: Network of hiking trails, shorter loop walks in Joyce Kilmer Forest; contact district forest ranger for detailed maps.

Directions: *Northwest 13.5 mi. from Robbinsville by SR 1127 to turn on USFS road 416 to trailheads and campground. Horse Cove campground located within .5 mile of Joyce Kilmer Forest on SR 1134.*

Ownership: USFS (704-479-6431)

Size: 16,932 acres   **Closest Town:** Robbinsville   P 🏠 🛖 ⛰ 🚶

91

Description: Largest wilderness area in Southern Appalachians. Rugged topography with deep valleys and steep ridges. Great variety of habitat types from cascading streams to ridgetop heath and grassy balds or spruce-fir forests. Tremendous diversity of plants and animals. Nearly 1,500 flowering plants including 150 tree species, and fifty-three fern species. More than 235 species of birds, thirty-five reptiles, thirty-nine amphibians, forty-six fish, seventy-one mammals, and many butterflies. Many species rare or widely separated from northern populations or endemic natives. Sanctuary for large mammals requiring extensive ranges like black bear and bobcat. Red wolf populations and five other animal species reintroduced. Designated world biosphere reserve.

Viewing Information: Many viewing opportunities from the cross-park Newfound Gap roadway and side roads, such as auto road to Clingman's Dome; periphery Foothills Parkway or Blue Ridge Parkway; Appalachian Trail (sixty-nine miles through park) or 850 miles of other hiking or horse trails, including more than fifty trails designated as "nature trails" or "quiet walkways."

Directions: Reached south of I-40 by any of several routes. Entered on North Carolina side usually by the Blue Ridge Parkway or from U.S. 441 through Cherokee Indian Reservation. Oconaluftee visitor center four miles north of Cherokee on Newfound Gap Road (U.S. 441), just west of Blue Ridge Parkway southern terminus.

Ownership: NPS (704-497-9146 or 615-436-1255)

Size: 520,004 acres, with 275,895 in North Carolina

Closest Towns: Cherokee in NC, Gatlinburg in TN

P🏕♿🌲🅰🚶

Black bears survive in large, undisturbed tracts of mountain forest and coastal wetlands. Only a lucky few will catch a glimpse of this secretive animal.
WILLIAM S. LEA

Additional Wildlife Viewing and Educational Opportunities

In North Carolina, wildlife may be seen and enjoyed in many locations—far more than can be described in a book of this size. The following organizations and publications have more information about wildlife in North Carolina:

North Carolina Museum of Natural Sciences, Raleigh (919) 733-7450

North Carolina Zoological Park, Asheboro (919) 879-5606

North Carolina Museum of Life and Science, Durham (919) 477-0431

Carolina Raptor Center, Charlotte (704) 875-6521

Discovery Place Science and Technology Museum and the Nature Museum, Charlotte (704) 372-6261

Dan Nicholas Park Nature Center, Salisbury (704) 636-2089

Highlands Nature Center, Highlands (704) 526-2602

Natural Science Center, Greensboro (919) 288-3769

Nature Science Center, Winston-Salem (919) 767-7630

Schiele Museum of Natural History, Gastonia (704) 864-3962

Western N.C. Nature Center, Asheville (704) 298-5600

North Carolina Nature Conservancy (919) 967-7007

National Audubon Society (919) 256-3779

North Carolina Division of Parks and Recreation, Raleigh (919) 733-4181

North Carolina Division of Coastal Management, Raleigh, (919) 733-2293

North Carolina Division of Forest Resources, Raleigh, (919) 733-2162

Aquariums in North Carolina

Fort Fisher, Kure Beach (919) 458-8257

Pine Knoll Shores, Atlantic Beach (919) 247-4003

Roanoke Island, Manteo (919) 473-3493

North Carolina Division of Forest Resources Educational Forests

Bladen Lakes State Forest, Elizabethton (919) 588-4161

Clemmons State Forest, Clayton (919) 553-5651

Holmes State Forest, Hendersonville (704) 692-0100

Rendezvous Mountain State Forest, Wilkesboro (919) 667-5072

Tuttle State Forest, Lenoir (704) 758-5645

Other Publications

A Directory to North Carolina's Natural Areas N.C. Natural Heritage Foundation. Raleigh, 1988. Description of natural habitats of the state and more than 100 exemplary sites.

State Parks of North Carolina Walter C. Biggs, Jr., and James F. Parnell. John F. Blair, Publisher, Winston-Salem, NC. 1989. Detailed guide to all state parks with maps.

Sierra Club Naturalist's Guide to The Piedmont Michael A. Godfrey. Sierra Club Books, San Francisco. 1980. Natural history of the Piedmont region in the Mid-Atlantic states.

Wildlife in North Carolina A monthly magazine published by the North Carolina Wildlife Resources Commission.

Popular Wildlife Viewing Species in North Carolina—And Where To Find Them

American alligator

Infrequently seen residents of freshwater streams and swamps of the southern and central coastal region. Croatan Pocosin Wilderness Areas and Lakes, Waccamaw Lake and River, Gull Rock Game Land.

Bald eagle

Populations rebuilding; more often seen soaring over lakes and rivers of Piedmont and coastal regions while hunting. Jordan Lake, Lake Mattamuskeet National Wildlife Refuge, Gull Rock Game Land, Raven Rock State Park.

Beaver

Generally found in small streams, ponds, and swamps; best seen near twilight or dawn. Merchants Millpond State Park, Durant Nature Park, Falls Lake, Blue Ridge Parkway: Moses Cone and Julian Price Parks.

Black bear

Secretive, seldom seen; inhabits large undisturbed tracts of forest in the coastal and mountain regions. Croatan Pocosin Wilderness Areas and Lakes, Holly Shelter Game Land, Bladen Lakes Educational State Forest, Joyce Kilmer Memorial Forest - Slickrock Wilderness, Great Smoky Mountains National Park, Alligator River National Wildlife Refuge.

Brown pelican

Frequently seen patrolling coastal shorelines while searching for fish. Fort Fisher State Recreation Area, Cape Hatteras National Seashore, Cape Lookout National Seashore, Hammocks Beach State Park

Canada geese

Most abundant wintering and year-round goose species in North Carolina. Mattamuskeet National Wildlife Refuge, Pea Island National Wildlife Refuge, Cowans Ford Wildlife Refuge and Latta Plantantion Park, Pee Dee National Wildlife Refuge.

Common raven

Larger than crow; frequently seen soaring over mountain crags enjoying wind currents. South Mountains State Park, Pilot Mountain State Park, Grandfather Mountain, Blue Ridge Parkway, Great Smoky Mountains National Park.

Fox squirrel

Watch for distinctive silver and black markings; inhabits mature pine forests of southern coastal plain region. Sandhills Game Land, Fort Bragg Army Installation, Raven Rock State Park, Weymouth Woods Preserve.

Golden eagle

Occasionally seen during late fall migrations on coast and mountains. Lake Mattamuskeet National Wildlife Refuge, Roan Mountain, Blue Ridge Parkway: Graveyard Fields.

Gray fox

Prefers forests more than open areas; hunts primarily rodents and rabbits, also eats fruit. Generally throughout the state. Jockey's Ridge State Park, Roanoke River Bottomlands, Mason Farm Biological Reserve, Stone Mountain State Park and Chatham Game Land, Green River Game Land.

Loggerhead sea turtles

Most frequently seen of the five Atlantic sea turtles; emerges from ocean to dig nest on undeveloped beaches at night in early summer. Bald Head Island, Hammocks Beach State Park, Masonboro Island, Cape Hatteras National Seashore.

Northern flying squirrel

Infrequently seen near twilight in high-elevation mountain forests. Grandfather Mountain, Mount Mitchell and Black Mountains, Roan Mountain.

Osprey

Most often seen flying low over shorelines of lakes and coastal waters while hunting for fish; stick nests are seen in lone trees along shoreline. Cape Hatteras National Seashore, Hammocks Beach State Park, Mattamuskeet National Wildlife Refuge, Cowans Ford Wildlife Refuge and Latta Plantation Park.

Peregrine falcon

Fall migrant seen hunting in coastal areas; population of year-round residents increasing in mountain region. Pea Island National Wildlife Refuge (migrants), Linville Gorge and Falls, Grandfather Mountain.

Red-cockaded woodpecker

Lives in colonies in open stands of old pine forest in coastal plain region; cavity trees marked by white sap running from nest holes and trees usually banded. Croatan Pocosin Wilderness Areas and Lakes, Millis Road Savanna, Patsy Pond, Holly Shelter Game Land, Bladen Lakes Educational State Forest, Jones Lake State Park, Fort Bragg Army Installation, Sandhills Game Land, Weymouth Woods Preserve.

Red fox

Most often seen of the wild canids; prefers open fields to woodlands; hunts primarily mice and rabbit. Generally throughout the state. Sandhills Game Land, Hanging Rock State Park, Stone Mountain State Park and Chatham Game Land, Linville Gorge and Falls.

Ruffed grouse

Game bird of mountain region; watch for in deep forests, wooded margins, and open meadows; listen for resonant "drumming" sounds. South Mountains

State Parks, Blue Ridge Parkway, Mount Pisgah, Standing Indian Mountain and Nantahala River Wetlands, Great Smoky Mountains National Park.

Snow geese
Large numbers of wintering birds found in refuges of northern coastal region. Pea Island National Wildlife Refuge, Mackay Island National Wildlife Refuge, Mattamuskeet National Wildlife Refuge, Pettigrew State Park and Lake Phelps.

Tundra swan
Large numbers of wintering birds found in refuges of northern coastal region. Pea Island National Wildlife Refuge, Mackay Island National Wildlife Refuge, Mattamuskeet National Wildlife Refuge.

Vultures, turkey and black
Often seen throughout state as they soar in search of carrion food or wind currents. Crowders Mountain, Pilot Mountain State Park, Linville Gorge and Falls.

White-tailed deer
Practically in all woodland tracts across entire state in large numbers; best seen in late afternoon or early morning near margins of forest and open fields. Lake Mattamuskeet National Wildlife Refuge, Goose Creek State Park, Ft. Bragg Army Installation, Hanging Rock State Park, Uwharrie National Forest, Cowans Ford Wildlife Refuge and Latta Plantation Park, Stone Mountain State Park and Chatham Game Land, Blue Ridge Parkway: Graveyard Fields.

Wild turkey
Populations rebuilding in large tracts of mature forests; best seen near dawn and twilight near margins of woodlands and open fields. Roanoke River National Wildlife Refuge, Caswell Game Land, Eno River State Park, Stone Mountain State Park and Chatham Game Land, Blue Ridge Parkway, Standing Indian Mountain and Nantahala River Wetlands.

Wood duck
A strikingly beautiful year-round resident; seen along streams and lakeshores. Nags Head Woods, Roanoke River National Wildlife Refuge, Cliffs of Neuse River State Park, Waccamaw Lake and River, Lumber River, Jordan Lake, Pee Dee National Wildlife Refuge.

Additional major types of species
Freshwater shellfish
Most imperiled group of animals, in massive population declines due to water pollution. Waccamaw Lake and River, Lumber River, Eno River State Park.

Marine birds
Abundant along coastal shorelines. Cape Hatteras National Seashore, Cape Lookout National Seashore, Hammocks Beach State Park, Fort Fisher State Recreation Area, Fort Macon State Park.

Marine invertebrates
Look in tidepools and salt marshes of coast. Fort Fisher State Recreation Area, Hammocks Beach State Park, Fort Macon State Park, Rachel Carson Estuarine Research Reserve, Cape Lookout National Seashore, Cape Hatteras National Seashore.

Migrating Raptors
Hawks and owls can be seen year-round throughout the state; larger numbers seen moving down coastline and Blue Ridge Mountain ridges during their fall migration from the north. Cape Hatteras National Seashore, Mattamuskeet National Wildlife Refuge, Cedar Island National Wildlife Refuge, Pilot Mountain State Park, Mount Jefferson State Park, Grandfather Mountain, Blue Ridge Parkway: Graveyard Fields, Whiteside Mountain.

Salamanders
Watch for in damp forests, in permanent water pools and ponds, rock crevices. Nags Head Woods, Sandhills Game Land, Hemlock Bluffs Nature Preserve, Durant Nature Park, Grandfather Mountain, Joyce Kilmer Memorial Forest—Slick Rock Wilderness, Great Smoky Mountains National Park.

Shorebirds
Found at any season along beach shorelines or tidal mudflats and sand bars in sounds. Baldhead Island (sandpipers), Hammocks Beach State Park, Cape Lookout National Seashore (piping plover), Rachel Carson Estuarine Research Reserve, Cape Hatteras National Seashore.

Wading birds
Generally seen in most sites on shorelines of rivers, ponds, marshes. Waccamaw Lake and River, Roanoke River Bottomlands, Falls Lake, Duke Power, Nags Head Woods, Merchants Millpond State Park, Lumber River, Cowans Ford Wildlife Refuge and Latta Plantantion Park.

Wintering ducks, loons, and cormorants
Abundant during winter migrations to coastal and piedmont waters. Cape Hatteras National Seashore, Pea Island National Wildlife Refuge, Mattamuskeet National Wildlife Refuge, Mackay Island National Wildlife Refuge, Goose Creek Game Land, Cowans Ford Wildlife Refuge and Latta Plantation Park.

Woodland songbirds
Found in nearly all sites. Carolina Beach State Park, Theodore Roosevelt Natural Area, Dismal Swamp National Wildlife Refuge, Roanoke River Bottomlands, Millis Road Savannah, Harris Lake, Moses Cone and Julian Price State Parks, Great Smoky Mountains National Park.

More Books From Falcon Press

The *North Carolina Wildlife Viewing Guide* is part of the Watchable Wildlife Series from Falcon Press. This series has been created through the National Wildlife Viewing Program, a Watchable Wildlife partnership initiative coordinated by Defenders of Wildlife. If you liked this book, look for the companion guides that cover other states you plan to visit.

In addition to the Watchable Wildlife Series, Falcon Press specializes in full-color nature books, calendars, and recreational guidebooks. If you want to know more about hiking, fishing, scenic driving, river floating, or rockhounding in your favorite state, check with your local bookstore or call toll-free 1-800-582-2665. When you call, please ask for a free catalog listing all the books and calendars available from Falcon Press.

Falcon Press Publishing Co., Inc.,
P.O. Box 1718, Helena MT 59624